Southern
Style

MARK MAYFIELD *with the* EDITORS *of* Southern Accents

Southern Style

A Bulfinch Press Book

Little, Brown and Company

Boston · New York · London

AUTHOR'S NOTE: This book includes the work of dozens of writers, photographers, and editors who have one common goal—to share with you the beauty and tastefulness of the South's interiors, architecture, and gardens.

Chief among those who labored over these pages is Frances MacDougall, senior editor for *Southern Accents* and in-house editor for *Southern Style*. The book simply would not have been possible without her many hours of writing, editing, and hard work. Other *Southern Accents* editors also contributed greatly, including Lindsay Bierman, Karen Carroll, and Karen Irons, who produced the core material for the magazine, as well as the writing and editing talents of Philip Morris, Candace Schlosser, Julie Cole, Lydia Longshore, and Heather Gibson. Freelance writers Liz Seymour and Andrea Oppenheimer Dean also made major contributions. I enjoyed writing for this book as well, particularly because it gave me an opportunity to pull back from the day-to-day management of the magazine and to examine and enjoy all that is so wonderful about Southern design and style.

Special thanks to former *Southern Accents* editor Katherine Pearson for her unwavering support and counsel, and to Carol Judy Leslie, vice president and publisher of Bulfinch Press, for her committment to this project. And my sincere thanks as well to Dorothy Williams, senior editor at Bulfinch, for her outstanding efforts on our behalf.

—Mark Mayfield

FRONTISPIECE: *French doors establish a graceful and unassuming entrance to this newly restored 1915 Dallas home. A silk-draped center table provides an intimate focal point in the grand foyer, where the owner's ever-changing arrangement of blue-and-white porcelain encourages guests to linger and admire.*

OPPOSITE: *While magnolia tree blossoms are short-lived, they can transform a simple floral arrangement in early May into a sumptuous symbol of Southern heritage.*

Copyright © 1999 by Southern Accents Magazine

Picture credits appear on page 206

First edition

Library of Congress Cataloging-in-Publication Data
Mayfield, Mark.
    Southern style / Mark Mayfield with the editors of Southern Accents.—1st ed.
        p.   cm.
    Includes index.
    ISBN 0-8212-2611-8
        1. Interior decoration—Southern States—History—
            20th century—Themes, motives.   I. Southern accents.
    NK2004.M39   1999
    747.215—DC21   99-11138

Book design by Evelyn C. Shapiro

Bulfinch Press is an imprint and trademark of Little, Brown and Company (Inc.)

PRINTED IN SINGAPORE

Contents

7   Introduction

17   CHAPTER I   Living Spaces

49   CHAPTER II   Dining Areas

75   CHAPTER III   Sleeping Areas

99   CHAPTER IV   Accessories

131 CHAPTER V   Architecture

155 CHAPTER VI   Gardens

179 CHAPTER VII   Preservation

196 Southern Historic Homes
198 Resources
202 Southern Museums
205 Acknowledgments
206 Picture Credits
207 Index

Introduction

Time has changed us, of course. We are, by and large, a far-flung, fast-moving and affluent people now, and they call us, not the South, but the Sunbelt. But here is a truth: Look into a Southern heart and there at its core, in the secret place where we have our beings, you will find the roots of home.
—Anne Rivers Siddons, "Landmarks"

FOR TWO CENTURIES, WRITERS HAVE BEEN TRYING TO CAPTURE the essence of the American South in novels, poems, essays, and long works of nonfiction. Many of these narratives—some of them much celebrated, like Harper Lee's *To Kill a Mockingbird* and Pat Conroy's *The Prince of Tides*— have not only captured the region's powerful sense of place, they have also exposed the dirty little secrets that always seem to lie somewhere just below the surface in both the rural and the urban South. Such is the Southern mystique, actually: the South is not only a land of hospitality and beauty, it is also an imperfect world, still, as it were, a work in progress.

Yet the South is moving on from its past sins and today retains the best of what has always been good about the region—its style and graciousness, two lofty attributes that are more important than ever at a time when technology rules. In the South at least, fine design and comfort have always taken precedence over technological marvels. That's not to say that we don't embrace modernism. Many of the interiors you see now in the pages of *Southern Accents* have contemporary furnishings and art, yet they have a tastefulness that is right out of the history books. Good taste, like great style, is never out of fashion.

Thomas Jefferson championed classical architecture as the appropriate expression for the new American republic, and he spent much of his life designing and rebuilding his beloved Monticello on its hill near Charlottesville, Virginia, as a model.

The outbuildings behind Charleston's historic Aiken-Rhett mansion are stark reminders of a side of the past that was very much a part of life, tragic as it was, in the antebellum South. Nearly twenty slaves once lived in the second-story quarters that face the stables at the house. "It is easy to find records of life in the South's big houses. Intact slave quarters, with all they can tell us, are much rarer," says Thomas Savage, former curator of the Historic Charleston Foundation.

It has not always been this way, this notion of a style so identifiable with a single region of America. At least it didn't start this way. The first European settlers on the North American continent had a far different style than the one that eventually would take hold, probably forever, in the South. Their furniture was coarse and uncomfortable, their lives were severe by necessity as well as by religious preference. They had to put their energy into simply surviving in a new world rather than into making their houses resemble the finer homes that some of them had left behind in Europe. Fortunately, "smart Southern style," as we define it today, has evolved over the years from sparse, even cold, formality, to relaxed, eclectic, embracing, and gracious interiors with taste, and yes, sophistication, that can hold their own against the ever-changing fads of New York and California.

What is Southern style? Perhaps it is easier to specify what it is not: trendy, campy, intimidating, or pretentious. On the contrary, it is a style that is accessible, incorporates the best in fabrics and furniture design, includes objects of sentimental value along with objects of great worth, and remains—always—grounded in the past. Our sense of history and respect for tradition have led to a relaxed attitude toward the use and display of fine furniture, antiques, and accessories. In essence, we live with the things that make us comfortable and secure. We value beauty, culture, education, and good conversation, along with a great bottle of wine now and then, and yes, we'll admit, a little gossip, too, from time to time. These are also qualities that we enjoy sharing with visitors who come to our region. The Southern expertise at entertaining, a natural extension of hospitality, has been handed down over generations, much like many of our furnishings and stately houses.

We also benefit greatly from a temperate climate, a sunbelt of weather that nurtures healthy, colorful gardens. These gardens have become extensions to our houses, and conversely, the colors and patterns of the gardens permeate our interiors.

Today there is a New South that attracts the attention of the world to cities like Atlanta, Dallas, Washington, D.C., Charlotte, New Orleans, and Charleston. The South may be a region distinct from the rest of the country, but its tastes and flair for restrained drama are now being imitated throughout America. Says Richard Keith Langham, a New York–based designer who was born and raised in Brewton, Alabama: "There were a number of very stylish houses in Brewton. They inspired me to do what I do. Even if I'm working in the most elegant of rooms, I bear in mind creature comforts and livability. I'd say that's a Southern thing. I know sweeping generalities are crazy, but I do think Southerners really know how to live."

Despite their disrepair, the doorways and windows to the Aiken-Rhett outbuildings lend an almost Gothic quality to what was once a bustling center of activity on the property. Repairs would not only have been too expensive but would also probably have hindered archaeological investigation of the grounds. Paint, plaster, brick, and timber yield clues to the social structure of a slave-holding household.

Perhaps it was Thomas Jefferson who first began defining what would later become known as Southern style. Whether your tastes are contemporary or traditional, fine or funky, if you're Southern, you tip your hat to classicism. And there is no better example in America for residential classicism than the house that started it all—Jefferson's Monticello. Nestled on the crest of a hill in Charlottesville, Virginia's rolling landscape, Monticello was a work in progress for much of Jefferson's life. He kept defining and redefining it for forty years, leaving us with a house that owes its inspiration to Andrea Palladio but took on Jefferson's own idiosyncrasies, including low-slung wings with terraced roofs that afford gorgeous views of the Charlottesville landscape. The relationship to the land and gardens drove Jefferson's unending search for a better way to design a home.

The same sense of place inspired the design of Charleston, South Carolina's Aiken-Rhett House, a masterpiece of Greek Revival style that today sits largely unrestored, a haunting and beautiful letter from a vanished world. Built in 1817 by Charleston merchant John Robinson, the house and its outbuildings were acquired in 1826 by William Aiken, a wealthy Charleston resident, who passed the property on to his son, William Aiken Jr. The younger Aiken and his wife, Harriet, furnished the great house with French wallpaper, enormous mirrors, chandeliers suspended from molded plaster ceilings, and European art purchased during a Grand Tour.

Later heirs found the estate too expensive to maintain, and gradually the grand rooms fell into disrepair. Today the house, despite its torn and frayed empty rooms and tarnished fixtures, is a reminder of how much the past plays a role in Southern interiors. Nineteenth-century diarist Mary Boykin Chestnut praised the "noiseless, automatic service" in the Aiken household, yet the worn stairs and shadowy spaces of the mansion's outbuildings, which housed slaves, are reminders that such service came at too great a price.

Nevertheless, the Aiken-Rhett estate is a lesson in the Southern sense of place. There is a spirit to the land that can never be altered by deterioration of a wall here, and a roof there. Some things go on forever. Read the words of one of the country's greatest living writers, Eudora Welty, in her essay "Some Notes on River Country": "A place that ever was lived in is like a fire that never goes out. It flares up, it smolders for a time, it is fanned or smothered by circumstance, but its being is intact, forever fluttering within it, the result of some original ignition. Sometimes it gives out glory, sometimes its

ABOVE: *Fireplaces still bear the soot of fires that once blazed at the Aiken-Rhett House. The aged colors of the walls lend a painterly quality to a bygone era.*

OPPOSITE: *Its walls and wall coverings torn and frayed by time, the living room of the Aiken-Rhett House nevertheless offers a glimpse of a golden past when entertaining was a way of life.*

little light must be sought out to be seen, small and tender as a candle flame, but as certain."

But like a flame, some traditions can eventually burn out. The most important room in a Southern home, for instance, used to be the formal living room, or parlor. It usually was a place for adults only, children allowed only under the closest supervision. To be sure, the chairs and sofas would be outfitted in beautiful fabric and the room itself was always decorated to the hilt, but most of us who sat in our Sunday clothes in these rooms were about as comfortable as teenagers on a blind date. We had to be on our best behavior, and even then there was always the chance of knocking over a prized figurine, or scratching a precious antique. And God help us if we ever dropped anything on the rug.

Fortunately for all of us, the latest trend has brought a wonderfully relaxed, approachable atmosphere to Southern living rooms. We actually "live" in them now, often even furnishing them with splendid antiques that are meant to be used, not just polished. And kids are allowed.

While the formal living room is a thing of the past, formal dining rooms are still very much in vogue. And for a simple reason: there is more formal entertaining in the South than anywhere else in America. And to promote conversation, large round tables are making a comeback in dining rooms, eliminating the question of who sits at the head of the table and giving everyone the chance to interact in a way that standard tables don't allow. Architects are also designing dining rooms near the entrance foyer, as if to say, "Come in, sit down, enjoy a meal with us."

The same conversational qualities of the living and dining rooms have now found their way to our kitchens as well. Home builders in the South will tell you that prospective homeowners are looking for larger kitchens with informal dining areas. After all, if you think about it, most of us spend an inordinate amount of time in our kitchen, and not just eating, but relaxing, talking on the phone, making notes, planning our day. In the days of the Aiken-Rhett household, the kitchens were always located in an outbuilding (for the good reason that there was no air-conditioning yet and the ovens generated a lot of heat, as well as sparks that could start a fire). Today, of course, our kitchens are integrated into our homes, and especially our dining areas, as many Southern families make an effort to eat together at breakfast and dinner.

The most private rooms in a Southern house are ironically usually its most decorative ones—the sleeping areas. While master bedrooms can some-

ABOVE: *The only daylight slaves working in interior rooms saw came through windows in a narrow corridor in the outbuildings.*

OPPOSITE: *The entrance hall of the Aiken-Rhett House, with its grand staircase, was typical of Southern mansions, where guests were welcomed with regularity.*

times err on the side of self-indulgence and convenience, guest bedrooms are the ultimate display of comfort and hospitality. Here a visitor is likely to find monogrammed linens, antique and heirloom furniture, classic colors, and plush textures.

Many of the accessories or furnishings in bedrooms, and beyond, are among collections that have been passed down from generation to generation. The past is still alive in today's interiors. Assembling a collection of art, antiques, photography, or any other decorative accessory is often the pastime of Southern homeowners. Many households have the luxury of adding to an existing collection that once belonged to ancestors. That is not to say that collectors aren't born every day in the South. After all, many of today's younger Southerners are more interested in abstract, modern art than their parents, and it's a good bet they'll hand down fine collections of contemporary art to their children. No longer are walls lined simply with family portraits or landscapes. Contemporary art plays a vital role here, and mixes well with eclectic interiors.

One tradition has never changed across the South. The weather makes it possible to sit outside nearly year-round, a major reason so many homes have grand porches and terraces. It is not surprising, then, that an open, flowing relationship exists between the homes and their gardens. Garden rooms thrive across the South, making it possible to bring nature inside, and just as possible to take furniture outside. Southern style carries seamlessly from interior to exterior and vice versa. Garden rooms, loggias, sunrooms, and greenhouses are commonplace. And outdoors, "rooms" are created in gardens with furniture, arbors, and statuary.

It is all part of the grand Southern experience of celebrating the land and its people, of living life as if every day counts, and of having pride in the past while admitting its injustices and inequities. In essence, writes Eudora Welty, in "Some Notes on River Country": "I have never seen...anything so mundane as ghosts, but I have felt many times there a sense of place as powerful as if it were visible and walking and could touch me."

CHAPTER I

Living Spaces

It is a nice little room too, with a low roof that slopes up to a point at the top and the prettiest wallpaper featuring a trellis design covered all over in the most beautiful morning glories you can possibly imagine. They are a deep purply blue, and the trellis is white, it is lovely beyond belief.

—Lee Smith, *The Christmas Letters*

OPPOSITE & ABOVE: *The vibrant, ballgown-like fullness of red cotton damask draws the eye to views of the city from this Paris apartment. The owner, an interior design professor from Tallahassee, Florida, selected fabrics and furnishings that make reference to his own tropical origins, and yet are decidedly European in taste.*

THE ROOTS OF SOUTHERN HOSPITALITY RUN DEEP. In eighteenth-century Virginia and South Carolina, the James, the Santee, and the Cooper Rivers were bordered with handsome plantations; the year's calendar was filled with a round of extended visits and friendly parties. "Nothing is now to be heard of in conversation," wrote one visitor to a Virginia plantation in 1773, "but the Balls, the Fox-hunts, the fine entertainments. . . ."

Aristocrats designed their generously proportioned plantation homes with hospitality in mind. Drawing rooms, sitting rooms, parlors, entrance halls, solariums, and—in the grandest houses—ballrooms or "assembly rooms" provided plantation families with the backdrop for endless convivial entertainments. Northerners might seek out excitement in Boston, New York, or Philadelphia, but Southerners were content to devise their own pleasures. "Being so well seated at home," explained one observer, "they have no ambition to fill a metropolis." Southerners have, of course, long since filled many busy metropolises, and live in many varieties of homes, but a uniquely regional tradition of warmhearted hospitality survives. From the entry hall to the garden room, and from ceiling to floor, homes are always dressed in their company best.

17

ABOVE: *Patterned wall covering and mirrored niches make the living room of this small London flat seem larger by blurring its spatial boundaries. The owners, a creative Mississippi couple, display objects collected from around the world.*

OPPOSITE: *The owners of this Montgomery, Alabama, bungalow have transformed their back entrance into a space for gardening storage and flower arranging.*

Company best doesn't, however, mean stiff formality or forbidding perfectionism. Hoop skirts and parasols are things of the past, and associating Southern design with those relics of a century ago misses the spirit that makes the essence of style endure. Even when its elements are unmistakably fine, a contemporary room is surprisingly unpretentious and underplayed. One of the most delightful and universal characteristics of Southern decorating is the honored position that heirlooms, family pictures, and personal collections hold in even the dressiest of rooms.

In sometimes breathtakingly bold strokes, we break the rules, folding wildly disparate periods, styles, and idioms into a single comfortable mix that implicitly invites our guests not only into our homes, but also into our lives. Heirlooms need not mean polished silver or gleaming mahogany, and in fact, the finest eighteenth-century Southern antiques have become so rare that even families fortunate enough to inherit them hesitate to put them into everyday use. But our heritage is, in any case, much broader than the traditional image of the British-influenced Georgian Tidewater and Low Country

*Deep, cushiony uphol-
stered pieces are the
foundation of this Baton
Rouge living room. Side
tables of various heights
mean that guests never
have to reach far to put
down a book or a cup
of coffee.*

style. The South is Spanish Florida, French New Orleans, Mexican Texas,
the rich traditions of African-American culture, the cosmopolitan mix along
Mississippi's Delta; and Southerners—whether our roots are measured in
years or centuries—proudly make our own histories part of our living
spaces. In Palm Beach, the architecture tends toward the Spanish-inspired
designs of Addison Mizner, with windows that let in light and furniture that
reflects the wealth and sophistication of the winter retreat. New Orleans's
homes are filled with French antiques, Aubusson and Savonnerie rugs, and
a spirit that bears the marks of age and inheritance. Tuscan scale that has
evolved from Spanish Colonial style and melded with Mexican materials
pervades the architecture and interior design of Texas.

Fringed swaths of silk frame French doors in this living room near Charlottesville, Virginia. Elements from the garden, such as the stone sculpture in the corner and a terra-cotta pot on the side table, bring in the outdoors.

Here, interior decorating is closely tied to the exterior. The countryside, with its beautiful wild places, is never far away, which may be why our homes reflect such an abiding love for natural materials. Floors—wood, stone, or terra-cotta—are covered in antique weaves or sisal, or simply left bare. Worn and weathered antiques proudly show the marks of passing years in even the most formal of living rooms. Windows dressed in little more than a length or two of beautiful fabric admit the sun and frame ever-changing views of the landscape.

We instinctively decorate living spaces in ways that make guests feel at ease. We are not afraid of pretty rooms. Well-placed lights, flattering colors, and comfortable upholstery pay visitors a subtle compliment, letting guests know that they are not only welcome to come in, but they are also invited to stay awhile.

THE ENTRY

The entry hall has always been more than a mere walk-through. While inhabitants of early New England houses gathered for warmth around a central chimney, leaving space for hardly more than an architectural pause between the front door and the rest of the house, Southern houses had chimneys at either end of the structure and a wide central passage from front door to back. During the warm months, the central passage stayed open to the breezes—and unexpected visitors. (In Southern mountain cabins, the wide passage is called a dogtrot.) During the hottest part of the summer, families would eat, entertain, and sometimes even sleep in the airy entry hall.

In grander houses, the entry hall also served as a kind of office lobby, where visitors on business errands waited their turn to see the man or woman of the house. At Monticello, Thomas Jefferson furnished his roomy entrance hall with straight-backed Windsor chairs and, characteristically, a display of maps and mastodon bones.

Practicality aside, a well-proportioned entry hall, especially when it is graced with a beautiful staircase, can be one of the most elegant spaces in the house. We furnish our entries as though they were full-fledged rooms, decorated with collections, favorite art, and inviting seats that convey the message that whether or not you choose to sit, you are welcome to linger and admire.

OPPOSITE: The foyer of this Baltimore apartment serves also as a dining room for parties of ten. Classical columns and a false door beside the red-painted bedroom hall entry were added for symmetry and grandeur.

RIGHT: A skirted table in the foyer of this home near Charlottesville, Virginia, is topped by loose arrangements of flowers from the garden. A muted patina comes across with softly striped wall covering, chintz curtains, and antique marble flooring.

ABOVE: *An informal seat-ing arrangement conveys a warm welcome inside the front door to this Atlanta home. The calming neutral palette, informal mix of patterns, and fanciful combination of styles put arriving family and friends at ease.*

OPPOSITE: *In the gallery between the foyer and the garden of this Dallas home, an arrangement of spring flowers parades across a dining table.*

Entry halls are often visible from other rooms and vice versa, providing an easy flow—and visual coherence—from room to room. The color that dominates the living room, for instance, may be used as a secondary color in the entry. A motif used in the entry may be repeated in the dining room. Even the house's exterior architecture can be a source of inspiration, from classical details to organic accents.

By definition, the entry hall is a place where first impressions count. Effects that might be overwhelming in the living room or library seem just right here—the entry hall lends itself to a little drama. Patterned floors, either inlaid or painted; deep baseboards; chunky moldings; statement-making lighting fixtures; bold wallpaper; and decorative painting—the entry hall is the place to pull out the stops (one caveat: to keep the hall navigable, avoid clutter).

A handsome round table, especially if it is visible through the open front door, is a wonderful focal point positioned in the center of a large entry hall. The table, which can be dressed in elegant fabrics or left bare, provides a place for a single theatrical arrangement of flowers and greenery, a stack of books, a collection of candlesticks, or anything else that, in fine Jeffersonian tradition, merits display. Even a small table, shelf, or bench, where guests can rest keys or packages while they untangle themselves from winter coats and scarves, and a chair, for such unromantic tasks as taking off boots, are thoughtful additions.

A beautiful entry hall is never more welcome, or welcoming, than when it is dressed in its holiday best. At Christmastime, garlands of greenery and cascades of ribbon festoon staircases, windows sparkle with candles and twinkling lights, sprigs of holly and mistletoe hang from the doorways. If the hall is roomy enough, a tree can fit in the curve of the staircase, or stand proudly in the center of the hall. One Texas homeowner even had an outlet installed in the floor during a renovation so she could light her entry hall tree at Christmas. Whatever the season, a well-decorated entry hall offers a warm greeting to everyone who opens the front door.

THE LIVING ROOM

There was a time not so very long ago when living rooms were used for anything but living. Stiff and uninviting, decorated with rigid formalism and furnished with touch-me-not discomfort, the living room was the "best" room in the house in the worst sense of the word. No more.

We have taken the starch out of living rooms and replaced it with a relaxed version of formality that transcends—and often mixes—periods and styles. In a charming play of point and counterpoint, mahogany furniture rests atop sisal carpeting, family silver takes a place of honor on a weathered console, or a carved French chair is upholstered in cotton ticking stripe. Well suited to the characteristically Southern blend of tradition and sociability, the best living rooms are meant to be used and enjoyed.

A scalloped slipcover reveals the wood frame of a daybed in this Atlanta living room. The formality of the antiques is downplayed by the use of cotton ticking and checks.

Balloon shades and leaded mullions disguise the view of an alley from the library of this Baltimore apartment. Several seating areas make the library multifunctional for reading, writing, watching television, dining, and relaxing.

Southerners aren't afraid of a little wear. In fact, we embrace it. Soft edges, peeling paint, gently worn carpets, and wood softly patinated with age lend history to a room, and like books in a well-stocked library, they surround guests with stories waiting to be told. Often the stories are personal ones, as photographs of friends and family keep company with the finest art in many Southern living rooms.

The furniture is often of the antique variety. Whether the pieces are from France, England, or Italy, from China, Japan, or Indonesia, or even from Maryland, Virginia, or Texas, they will be as individual as their owners. The eighteenth century seems to get the most attention among collectors of European antiques, while Asian antiques could be four hundred to five hundred years old. Since our country is so young, most American antique tables, chairs, and beds date from the nineteenth century. The South even produced its own distinctive furniture, which includes huntboards, usually

ABOVE: *A wing chair
pulled up to a writing
table adds more comfort
to working at home or
paying bills. In this Baton
Rouge library, upholstered
walls and heavy curtains
muffle sound distractions.*

called Southern sideboards; lazy Susan tables; sugar chests; and cellarets, for storing libations—prized for their medicinal properties, of course.

The leisurely pace of Southern entertaining promotes good conversation, and we design our living rooms with that in mind: intimate seating groups help bring even the largest high-ceilinged rooms down to human scale. Furnished with comfortable sofas to sink into, lightweight chairs that can be drawn close to the center of talk, and ottomans that sometimes double as coffee tables, living rooms come alive.

Upholstered furniture is the foundation of any living room. Comfort need not be sacrificed for style. Generous proportions and deep, downy cushions look as beautiful as they feel, and even the most severely contemporary pieces often have their edges softened with pillows: cushy pillows, plump pillows, and Tootsie Roll–shaped bolsters for tucking into the small of your back.

Thoughtfully arranged side tables, coffee tables, and sofa tables mean that guests never have to reach far to put down a drink or a cup of coffee. Lately the old-fashioned tea table—or at least tables of tea table height—

ABOVE: *This London living room seems as if it would be as much at home in rural Virginia as it is in England. The designer is the granddaughter of one of the three famed Langhorne sisters of Charlottesville, Virginia, who took the world of English style and decorating by storm.*

OPPOSITE, BELOW: *Special lighting and an improvised stage created by the original hand-carved mantel make the owners' collection of blue-and-white Chinese porcelain the center of attention in this Dallas living room.*

have made a comeback, placed in front of a sofa in lieu of a low coffee table. A little more formal than a conventional coffee table, a tea table also has the practical advantage of being easy to use without forcing a guest, or host, to lean or stoop. Smaller tables—sculptural candle stands, painted and gilded demilunes, humble stools—do double duty as furniture and decorative accents.

The South is too big and too diverse to have a single palette, but many Southern living rooms are washed in the pale neutrals that seem to cool the region's warm climate. Some homeowners, particularly along the Gulf Coast where the West Indian influence is still strong, have gone so far as to revive the tradition of white summer slipcovers. Others evoke the fresh look of summer dressing year-round with natural linen and deep-breathing cotton upholstery.

The tranquil color mix relies on texture, not pattern, for its drama: in formal settings, velvets, tone-on-tone damasks, antique needlepoint, and crinkly silk. In more relaxed living rooms, linen, canvas, and aged leather do the trick. Together they create a rich, understated background that puts people where they belong—at the center of attention.

Color and pattern may be downplayed, but the living room is the place for architectural flourishes, improvised if necessary. When architectural details are awkward or, as they are in many new houses, absent, Southerners

BELOW: *This New Orleans sitting room may be full of great period pieces like a Louis XVI screen and nineteenth-century Barbedienne urns that serve as lamps, but according to the owner someone always ends up asleep on the velvet-covered, Knole-style sofas.*

OPPOSITE: *The silk upholstery on the Louis XV bergère will never go out of style.*

go for the dramatic gesture: an antique folding screen hung across one wall, a broad tapestry suspended from a wrought-iron rod, an oversized mirror in an elaborate frame filling the space from mantel to ceiling. Most major Southern cities have artisans who will convert bits of salvaged ironwork into useful new tables and consoles. Even used as-is, architectural fragments of metal, stone, or painted wood make bracingly bold accents in otherwise refined rooms.

Living room floors in the South tend to be dressed down with sisal or other natural fiber floor coverings, or dressed up with warm Oriental rugs. Turkish Oushaks, with their soft, sunny colors and worn pile, are a special Southern favorite. Families lucky enough to have polished hardwood floors frame their carpets in large borders of bare floor. Even wall-to-wall carpet is often treated as though it were simply another flooring material, with area rugs layered on top.

In the living room, where privacy becomes a secondary consideration in window dressing, sunlight slants through windows adorned with restraint. Classic panel draperies are the current favorite, interpreted in everything from barely-there sheers to billowing silk that sweeps the floor like a debutante ballgown. With such careful editing, every detail counts. Window hardware, from robust wooden rods with carved and painted finials to slender hand-forged iron rods, has become an important part of a room's jewelry, decorative accents in their own right.

A good living room, like a good party, is a masterpiece of careful planning, but as every experienced host or hostess knows, the nicest things often happen by chance. Filled with personal collections, invigorated with a mix of texture and materials, and enlivened with a sophisticated mix of ease and decorum, Southern living rooms are dressed and ready for every occasion, from a blue-jeaned cup of coffee to a black-tie nightcap. Living, like the living room itself, is too good to save for special occasions.

This New Orleans front parlor is in summer dress, and its shutter louvers are open to catch a river breeze. Behind the Natchez sofa, an American classical table holds a miniature armoire for dolls and a glass garden cloche.

The use of outdoor draperies, rather than indoor window treatments, appears to expand the space of this New Orleans living room onto the adjoining terrace.

THE FAMILY ROOM

"Family" is a highly elastic word in the South. In traditional Southern families, the family circle radiates outward in rings of relationships that include cousins, grandparents, nieces and nephews, and friends. Southern houses are much the same. The architect may have planned the family room as a members-only retreat, but the room has a way of becoming a handsome second sitting room, an intimate place for entertaining *en famille*—whoever the family happens, at the moment, to be.

Family rooms are descended from the whole range of rigidly defined libraries, morning rooms, and sitting rooms—both public and private—that a century ago were part of the South's grandest homes. Here at the end of the twentieth century, however, we have reverted to the habits of our eighteenth-century forebears, who used every room in the house for a multitude of purposes. Today the functions of the library, the sitting room, the game room (or its modern equivalent, the media room), and even the home office are often folded into a single hardworking space.

Family rooms, like families, evolve over time. As children grow older and eventually move away, the family room grows up, and the shock-absorbent furniture that makes sense in a household of young children and teenagers can be replaced with more sophisticated pieces. The fragile family heirlooms that were carefully tucked away in the attic or placed out of reach

RIGHT: *A young graphic designer converted her family's dairy barn near Baton Rouge into her own home and studio. The Acadian blankets, made of homespun cotton, are from her family's collection.*

BELOW: *This Washington, D.C., family room is dressed in solid chenilles and crewel curtains. The fabrics and furnishings are luxurious but shock-absorbent for a family with young children.*

ABOVE: *Sculptural pieces stand out in bold relief against the white walls of this home in Dallas. The textural grain of bare wood floors contrasts with the smooth, light-colored fabrics and materials.*

RIGHT: *Daylight floods this family room in Baton Rouge, which is enveloped in rich, earthy colors and patterns. The owner's collection of blue pottery, grouped on the coffee table, can easily be moved to the mantel, out of children's reach.*

ABOVE, LEFT: *An 1888 church window is a focal point in this cottage overlooking Lake Martin in Alabama. The statuesque lamp came from an old hotel lobby.*

ABOVE, RIGHT: *An antique book on the English pedestal table in the living room is opened to a drawing of a brown pelican, one of the owner's favorite birds from Mobile Bay, Alabama.*

can return to center stage. New interests find expression as parents of grown children discover more time to relax and explore. Eventually space is made on a table or wall for framed pictures of grandchildren in the family room.

Even when the family size has been pared back down to two, the family room is a welcome gathering place. We take these rooms seriously and dress them with the same care devoted to the living room, though the equation can be reversed. Where the living room is formal but relaxed, the family room is relaxed with just a touch of formality, the sort of room that can accommodate pizza for ten or cocktails for two. With that in mind, a small informal dining table (it can double as a game table for those so inclined) is a nice addition.

The color palette in the family room—and in its near-cousin, the library—is often richer and deeper than in the living room. Warm, saturated tones draw the walls in and the family circle closer. To keep the feeling serene, upholstery, window treatments, and floor coverings may pick up the color of the walls. Even red can be treated as a soothing neutral in an all-enveloping color scheme. Although upholstery and window treatment fabrics may be of very fine quality, they often have a more rough-hewn character than their equivalents in the living room—cotton instead of silk, or linen instead of damask.

Upholstered furniture in the family room is, almost by definition, plump, comfortable, and durable. Slipcovers make practical sense in the family room, as does leather, which only grows more beautiful with age. Nubby fabrics like chenille often have stain-resistant, man-made fibers blended in. Sturdy wood pieces, already reassuringly worn around the edges, can be dressed up or down with accessories. A mix of woods and finishes in the room reinforces a timeless sense of relaxation.

These rooms also work best with a sense of humor. While proportion counts in any good design, family room furniture and accessories can take a few liberties with balance and scale. Function rules: furniture may be positioned askew if that is the best way to capture a view of the television or fireplace. Casters show up on furniture that must be mobile. Oversized chairs,

An area rug from Santa Fe mixes well with French antiques in this one-room-wide Creole plantation house in Pass Christian, Mississippi. Windows are left bare on each side of the room to emphasize the connection of the interior to its flanking porches and gardens.

RIGHT & OPPOSITE:
The subtle palette of this house in Washington, D.C., was inspired by the colors of dried hydrangeas, the owner's favorite flowers.

PREVIOUS PAGE:
Bookcases in the study of a house on Mobile Bay in Point Clear, Alabama, hold a collection of nineteenth- and twentieth-century hat molds from French and American milliners.

chunky lamps, whimsical collections massed in unexpected ways, walls of silly family pictures or colorful children's art that would be out of place in the living room, give the family room its unique personality.

One "collectible" that no Southern home is without is books. The regional literary tradition that produced some of America's greatest writers also produced generations of readers. Even when a house has a formal library, books seem to find their way into the family room. Bookshelves, whether built-in or freestanding, can be beautiful accents on their own. Filled with literary volumes, they have commanding visual impact (aided by a little editing: ratty, much-read paperbacks should be shelved in a less visible part of the house). In dressed-down family room style, books also become part of the decorating scheme—a stack on a table can elevate a lamp or flower arrangement, a stack on the floor can serve as a low table.

The television has been the family room's electronic hearth since the 1950s, but today it is not only bigger, it also comes accompanied by a VCR, videotapes, speakers, and other electronic accoutrements. Whatever its size, however, home entertainment equipment need not dominate the room. All but the most elaborate projection televisions can be tucked into cabinetry or hidden behind closed doors in specially equipped armoires (experts warn, however, that any cabinet that will hold electronics should be well ventilated). An even simpler solution is to hide electronics behind a folding screen that can be easily moved aside when the evening news comes on.

But it is the other hearth—the real one—and the people who draw around it that truly warm a family room. Like the front porch in an earlier era, the family room is the place where stories are told, where advice is shared, and where generations spend time getting to know one another.

THE GARDEN ROOM

We have become so used to strawberries in winter and fresh flowers year-round that we have forgotten what a delightful luxury the conservatory once was. Warmed all winter by the sun's rays, the glassed-in conservatory provided the most fortunate Southerners with greenery, flowers, and fruit out of season when frost nipped the garden. Today the garden room is as much a cool retreat from the summer's heat as it is a winter haven. Inspired by eighteenth-century orangeries—and by more recent memories of screened-in porches—garden rooms bridge the distance between indoors and out.

Lately the loggia, an open-air version of the garden room, has become popular in some parts of the South, most particularly in Texas, where Tuscan-style architecture, well suited to the Texas climate, has taken root. When a loggia is deep enough to be protected from the elements, it can be furnished very much like an indoor room, with rugs on the floor, draperies, and cushy pillows (prudently filled with mildew-resistant stuffing). Wicker is a popular and appropriate choice for the loggia's indoor-outdoor feeling, but other, chunkier materials—iron, teak, and weathered pine—go particularly well with a loggia's traditional Mediterranean architecture.

OPPOSITE: *Blue-and-white porcelain combines with tiles on a stucco wall in Boca Grande, Florida. The warm climate and deep overhang allow the owners to put the antique daybed outdoors.*

RIGHT: *A curving wall of glass extends from one wall of a Washington, D.C., family room to create the feeling of dining in the garden year-round.*

ABOVE: *At one end of
a loggia in this Dallas
house, a sun-filled den
invites views of a creek
that divides the property's
gardens in two. The nat-
ural feel of the space is
enhanced by antelope-
patterned carpeting and
comfortable furnishings.*

OPPOSITE: *A mirror
hangs on the frame of the
window in this Atlanta
sunporch. Garden rooms
lend themselves to combi-
nations of floral and leaf
prints which appear on the
sofa, chairs, and pillows.*

A good garden room is also multifunctional, serving both indoors and
out. Artful design weaves the two elements together, avoiding botanical
clichés but evoking the landscape through allusion and subtle suggestion.
Flooring, for instance, often marks the transition from the other parts of the
house with slate, terra-cotta tile, or brick. Even humble concrete can be colored and patinated to look like much grander materials. Soothing, nature-
inspired colors on the walls invite the outdoors in. In some garden rooms,
trellises applied to the walls help to dissolve the spaces between windows,
giving them the illusion of transparency.

Cues from the landscape help to set the scene in a wide-windowed garden room or open-air loggia. Garden styles and architectural motifs, whether
formal or natural, classical or contemporary, can be carried over into a loggia or garden room. A garden room need not be filled with leafy upholstery
fabrics and traditional patio furniture to make the connection. Subtler cues—
an antique garden urn, floral-patterned pillows—hold their own without
competing with the view.

A garden room, often highly visible from other rooms of the house, may also echo some of the colors and themes that have been established elsewhere indoors. And conversely, a garden room can help to set design motifs for adjoining spaces. Indoor fabrics—cotton prints, linens, velvet—that are too perishable to use in the garden or even on a loggia, look lovely and inviting in the protected confines of a garden room. Outdoor ingredients, such as potted, flowering plants, are often mixed in with portable furniture in lightweight natural materials—wicker, rattan, and bamboo.

Parties have a way of spilling over into a comfortably furnished garden room or loggia. Just as in the living room, small and attractive tables—including, if space permits, one for intimate dining—make the areas all the more inviting. Candles and flattering lighting, which are lovely decorative elements on their own, carry the rooms beautifully into the night. To aid the transformation, a small cabinet can store table linens, silverware, and extra candles.

Part of the "garden" of any garden room or loggia comes from the container-grown plants it sustains. The containers themselves are important, bringing color, texture, and drama into a room. Always growing and changing, easy to rearrange or move out entirely—in fact, some garden room plants are happiest if they can spend the summer outdoors—plants keep a garden room dynamic.

Choices these days go way beyond the conventional ferns and pots of ivy. Miniature stands of bamboo, feathery palms, and tropical banana plants add a touch of exoticism and bold sculptural beauty that can become the most important statement in a room where nature—both indoors and out—plays the starring role.

On a smaller scale, groups of accessories add a warm and human dimension. The best collections are acquired over time and often come with stories attached—reminders of trips, interests, family, and friends. If they don't "go" together in the traditional sense, all the better: juxtapositions of style, materials, periods, and even value make collections all the more interesting.

CHAPTER II

Dining
Areas

If some wizard would like to make me a present, let him give me a bottle
filled with the voices of that kitchen, the ha ha ha and fire whispering, a bottle brim-
ming with its buttery sugary bakery smells. . . . It looked more like a cozy
parlor than a kitchen.

—Truman Capote, *The Grass Harp*

ABOVE: *Bean pods in
a pewter pitcher add
vitality to the long refec-
tory table and slipcovered
chairs and bench at this
lake house. Natural light
from the windows brings
out the patinas of the
various woods through-
out the room.*

OPPOSITE: *Contemporary
glassware, cobalt water
glasses, and whimsical
wineglasses create a traditional look when paired
with green-and-white
china. Several clusters of
wild roses are scattered
about the inlaid table.*

HAM FROM VIRGINIA, BEIGNETS FROM NEW ORLEANS, BARBECUE
from Birmingham—mention the South, and food naturally comes to mind.
Distinctive flavors are intimately tied to the region's character. Whether nou-
velle cuisine or down-home comfort food, an important part of the South's
history revolves around putting food on the table. Years ago, we spent much
of our time tending, preparing, and eating rich, distinctive dishes. Today,
most everyone has gradually become less consumed by the drudgeries of
tending and more consumed by the joys of eating. But the most basic needs
are necessarily universal, and in hunger we transcend years and generations,
evoking memories from long ago with something as simple as the aroma of a
freshly baked pecan pie, or perhaps the plate it is served upon. Our landscape and homes, of course, are settings for everyday dramas, where the
rooms associated with foods—the dining room, the kitchen—are cherished
places in which creative juices elevate nourishment and its accompaniments
to high art forms.

"The French have a saying that Americans talk about the weather and
the French talk about food. Well, I say they don't know about Southerners,"
says Edna Lewis, renowned cookbook author and Southern chef, who has

extolled the virtues of Southern cuisine for more than fifty years. Expect the unexpected in this region, where quirky details and little eccentricities add just the right spice to any dish. In the best dining rooms and kitchens, Southerners won't leave out essential elements, like, say, the sideboard. But we may just make that sideboard out of ornate ironwork from a New Orleans balcony. As with Scarlett O'Hara and her drapery dress, often the most unconventional pieces form a perfectly traditional whole.

So much of the region is steeped in the past, for better or worse. In its best manifestations, the link with days gone by enables us to make things that are old appear fresh and appealing by today's standards. The lines between the regions that separate New England from Midwest, South from West, are beginning to blur, and times are always changing, but some of the best of Southern traditions—like lingering over a special meal with family, gathering at the table to talk politics and gossip, bringing out the best to

ABOVE: *Etched glass, silver goblets, and silver candlesticks make an opulent table setting. Filling the antique silver epergne is an arrangement of roses, viburnums, and lilacs that is elaborate enough to be appreciated but not too tall to prevent conversation across the table.*

RIGHT: *Tradition gets updated in this Dallas dining room, with its hand-painted wallpaper and sumptuous window treatments. Though the windows, walls, and chairs are covered, the round table and wood floors are left bare. The contemporary chairs with caned backs feature animal-print upholstery for an eclectic look.*

The round table in this Virginia dining room is skirted in cotton-and-wool moiré and surrounded by Hepplewhite shieldback chairs with their original paint. Nineteenth-century Chinese watercolors flank an antique mirror over the settee against the wall.

make friends and visitors feel welcome—are ones we still honor. Yet we're not about to turn our backs on the revolution in labor-saving devices for the kitchen, so modern conveniences are honored too.

Other changes within the home have affected the kitchen's role profoundly. The dining room and kitchen, for instance, were once very disparate entities. The kitchen was simply a work area, a building separate from the rest of the house, not conducive to lounging, to say the least. It was where a great many of the household chores took place. The best of late eighteenth-century kitchens usually had dirt or brick floors to protect them from sparks from the large fire. They had high ceilings and big open windows to promote

ABOVE: *In an 1821 raised Creole cottage near New Roads, Louisiana, the windows are draped in Provençal cotton. The floors were laid with oversized bricks that were made on the plantation.*

OPPOSITE: *For a casual dining spot in Houston, a rusting chandelier throws soft light on neutral walls and slipcovered seating. A folding screen made of bas-relief ceiling tiles defines the space.*

cool crossbreezes and the quick dissipation of all the smells of smoking meat and other dishes. Kitchens were rough, coarse, utilitarian spaces, ones that would be wiped clean, swept out, and scrubbed often. They consisted of equipment and workspace and that was all. Of course, many things have changed for the better over the course of the last two hundred years.

In the dining room, progress hasn't been quite so thorough, fortunately. The best of late eighteenth- and nineteenth-century dining rooms were used more often than today's and for more than just dining, a trend that is gaining ground in Southern dining rooms once again. The dining room was a comfortable place where everyone gathered together to enjoy one another's company over dinner, to talk, to visit, to entertain. Over the years, the kitchen and the dining room have blended together somewhat, the kitchen with its informal dining spaces expanding to take on much of the dining room's former duties. But still, the dining room is its own treasured place in the South, and it too is expanding, opening itself up to new possibilities.

THE FORMAL DINING ROOM

It has become the vogue among some designers in the last few years to declare the dining room dead, but not so in the Southern home. The dining room has staked its claim here, and, like the kitchen, is expanding and evolving into a room that evokes tradition like no other.

Historically, the traditional Sunday dinner was a large affair, carefully planned each week, and prepared painstakingly in the kitchen for hours, if not days, beforehand, and marked by an abundance of meats, vegetables, breads, and desserts. Sunday dinner is not a romanticized fantasy, nor is it a throwback to yesteryear. Today, this weekly gathering may include more healthful and worldly approaches to eating. And it may include quick dishes or even takeout. But among many Southern families, Sunday dinner is still a ritual, a time to catch up, slow down, and connect to days past.

Nothing in the dining room is too precious to be used. All the props—the china, the silverware, the crystal—come out for the show. The most cherished, one-of-a-kind items are brought forth and offered up as unquestionably as a timeworn wooden biscuit bowl. Often the home of the most treasured of family heirlooms, the dining room helps keep family members connected to their lineage, whether through tangibles, such as antiques, or

RIGHT: *In this Washington, D.C., home, the Oushak rug inspired the folding screen's Moorish design. Dining chairs get dressed up to suit the striking setting, but simple goblets and a centerpiece of wild fruits and berries keep the room versatile enough for any kind of party.*

OPPOSITE: *Though the previous homeowner had furnished this immense Dallas dining room with a single long table, the current owner broke with tradition and used three round tables, dressed in silk and surrounded by heavy chairs with plump pillows. The lithograph is by Renoir.*

intangibles, like the mood and the food, carefully prepared using recipes handed down through generations.

Dining tables themselves come in a variety of shapes—from round to oval to rectangular—and sometimes just one table won't do. Of course, the round table is the most democratic of choices, designating neither head nor foot; at a round table, everyone can interact. But round tables require very large or square rooms, and often leaves to expand the surface in order to seat the maximum number of guests. While large, round antique tables are virtually impossible to come by, new handcrafted tables are taking over grand Southern dining rooms.

A rectangular table, on the other hand, seats more guests, can have more leaves, and does not necessarily require a room with gargantuan

BELOW: *The muted palette in this South Carolina house capitalizes on the warmth of the fire, natural light, a mirrored wall, and sisal flooring. A former restaurateur, the homeowner combines the subtle detailing of European hotel silver and George III–style chairs covered in a casual but tailored linen duck. Behind the formal, custom-painted table is an additional, more intimate seating area.*

RIGHT: *In an unusual arrangement, a silver tea service serves up a bouquet of roses atop a sideboard. The flowers are repeated in the floral wallpaper in the background.*

ABOVE: *This dining room fills the foyer of an 1850 house in Point Clear, Alabama, bidding welcome to all who enter. The three-pedestal English table is in a highly trafficked area and is elegantly framed by the main stairway. Sisal flooring and linen slipcovers give a relaxed formality to the room.*

RIGHT: *Old silver spoons, worn from age and use, are juxtaposed with antique creamware.*

proportions. The oval-shaped table has all the benefits of the rectangular table, but is often better suited to tight spaces, has soft edges, and inspires a flow that a rectangular table might interrupt. Of course, if space is not a problem, multiple tables in a room—whether of the same or varying sizes—provide the ideal solution.

Despite the seriousness of fine furniture, in the end all of the pieces that make up the dining room must be livable, inviting, and comfortable. Otherwise the dining room becomes intimidating and off-putting, sterile and overpreserved. This is where imagination and creativity breathe new life into the room. English Chippendale, French Louis XVI, or Chinese Ming chairs may be uniformly the same or they may be mismatched, out of appreciation for varying styles or as a reference to late eighteenth- and nineteenth-century dining rooms, where seating was pulled in from all areas to accommodate large groups of people at dinner. In the summer chairs are often slipcovered in crisp white fabric to try to turn down the heat a bit. Plush pillows may pad seats, or they may be bare, well-ventilated cane. Rugs are not a necessity,

A seventeenth-century statue of the apostle Paul watches over the open interiors in this house, inspired by the design of traditional country churches. The wood used in the bare floors was also used for the walls, creating a clean, unified space. The triptych in the kitchen is a beauty pageant photo of the owner's mother.

but when present, they're often sisal or sea grass, coarse and tightly woven to counterbalance the rigidity of massive, formal wood furniture. The mellow tones of soft Oriental rugs meld with the patina of centuries-old antiques. And floral arrangements are essential, but not the kind that appear frozen within some geometrical constraint. Loose sprays of wildflowers, multicolored hydrangea blossoms, grasses and twigs, single stems within many small bottles—these are the arrangements that add intrigue, color, and texture.

Although we love rich tradition and formality, the dining room is often the most dramatic space in the house precisely because it isn't used every day. Bold paint, furnishings, draperies, all add to the drama. Speckled mirrors that may lack some of their silvering radiate brilliance and glitter as they cast candlelight about the room. And chandeliers are big, full of the weight of their layers.

In contrast, the family's monogrammed napkins are understated. Carefully crafted tables need no coverings, but they come to life when laden with collections of vases, bibelots, and hydrangeas, magnolias, and grasses. Unusual uses of dramatic pieces help define the look of the dining room. For despite heaps of antiques and precious trinkets, it is their unexpected use that creates a truly inspired room—one that feels fresh and new, not like a studied, regimented museum display. Mustard jars become vases; a table base is fashioned from an old wood column; a grid of painted bas-relief ceiling tiles becomes a screen.

INFORMAL DINING AND THE KITCHEN

The informal dining spaces in the Southern home are often right within the kitchen. The utilitarian work surface of the late eighteenth- and nineteenth-century kitchen has evolved into today's kitchen table, where family members congregate for more than breakfast, lunch, and dinner. These informal dining areas are most frequently decorated with a relaxed, rustic touch. Appealing, but tough enough to withstand the rigors of daily use, the spaces are marked with the coarse textures of sisal or woven cotton area rugs atop hardwood flooring, rush seats and baskets, timeworn tables, and chunky pottery. Eclectic collections of transferware pottery, wildflowers, and a hodgepodge of chairs accumulated over the years may find their way into the everyday dining area.

Dining room fabrics may pull out all the stops with rich dramatic tones. The textures and shades of neutral fabrics may mimic the patina of

RIGHT: *Despite the fact that the formal dining area is just next door, a collection of plates in the breakfast room ranges from dime-store finds to Staffordshire. The area features a variety of patterns; the black-and-white color palette unifies the space. Metal palm trees and statuary provide the centerpiece.*

OPPOSITE: *The earthy palette for this Birmingham kitchen is based on the needs of a couple with young children. Matte stone floors complement the concrete counters. Black moldings around windows and doors match the picture frames. The weighty table is visually lightened with a variety of chairs.*

ABOVE: *The homeowners, architects in Montgomery, designed the island and vinyl benches for the kitchen in their bungalow. They found the chandelier in a St. Louis theater and framed the doorway with sixteenth-century wooden panels. A green lizard stencil pattern skirts the ceiling.*

RIGHT: *Antique tiles envelop the work island at this San Antonio ranch, which evokes the raw essential classicism of old Texas missions. A hearth inspired by pioneer kitchens frames a modern commercial range.*

BELOW: *For this innovative dining area within the kitchen, an oval table is surrounded by a banquette and contemporary pineapple-backed chairs that extend a welcome.*

RIGHT: *A collection of early nineteenth-century pottery and porcelain, including some pieces excavated from the property of this Louisiana house, is kept behind the glass doors of a cypress cabinet.*

A fireplace and book-shelves add coziness to an oblong French cherry table found in New Orleans. Chairs from Hong Kong have been cushioned with old ticking.

old cabinetry and furniture. In a not-so-formal eating area, less serious motifs and colorways create a vibrant mix with other collections of table-ware and artwork. Printed and patterned cotton and linen fabrics may be more suited to everyday wear, but that doesn't mean we must sacrifice aesthetic appeal for the sake of durability. Here, too, loose slipcovers stick around year-round because they can be easily removed and laundered.

These rooms often feature a variety of eating spots, such as banquettes and bars in addition to the basic table. In fact, the informal dining area is a spot that the whole family gravitates toward. The table, which is not just a place to eat, also becomes a place to do homework, to plan menus, to spread out the Sunday paper and linger over coffee. Usually connected to if not within the kitchen, this place is often the hub of family activity.

A scratched and scarred antique table may be enjoyed as much today in Charlotte as it was, years ago, in the Provençal countryside where it was first crafted and used on a daily basis. A wrought-iron candelabra will evoke a Mexican repast; bamboo candlesticks lend a distinctly Asian flair. And no overriding theme seems ever to prevail. Georgia pottery mingles with Japanese porcelain; odd pieces of silver flatware, worn from years of use and perhaps monogrammed with a variety of initials, appear right at home with eclectic dinnerware.

The kitchen itself has changed much over time. Once a separate structure where only the work of cooking took place, the kitchen moved into the main house and invited everyone to take a seat. This is where the members of the household meet for a morning cup of coffee, a glass of orange juice, or a sneak peek at platters filled with pancakes and eggs, bacon, and biscuits on their way to the table. It's the place to unwind over a glass of wine, grab a quick snack before dinner. And in its most marked departure from kitchens of decades past, the kitchen attracts many guests during formal and informal parties. In fact, everyone ends up in the kitchen, so it is decorated like any other room in the house, with antiques, comfortable chairs, artwork, and flattering lighting that supplements the ugly overhead lighting of decades past.

In this 1950s brick ranch in the woods of South Carolina, the kitchen is a room for socializing. It has multiple seating areas. The modern refrigerator and traditional oven make this a luxurious workspace.

But that's not to say that the room doesn't see its share of work. As in kitchens past, vital chores are still accomplished here. Today's homeowners like to seek out the best in appliances, buying professional stoves and ovens, state-of-the-art refrigerators and dishwashers. Modern conveniences can be luxurious and still inspire creativity. Rustic painted tiles, ironwork, and pottery, all wrought by hand, add age and character to improve the cool, sleek lines of professional appliances and utensils. Multiple refrigerators placed in a few strategic work areas eliminate some of the hustle and bustle. Plenty of shelving and cabinetry keeps necessities close at hand. Our kitchens may be indulgent, but they are efficient too.

Often connected to the garden, kitchens take advantage of its bounties, be they figs, peaches, basil, or thyme. An affinity for the land runs deep in

Shade plants surround this Palm Beach paradise. The versatile rear terrace serves as an outdoor living or dining room.

ABOVE: *Vibrant colors have an Old World feel at this table setting in Dallas, where Victorian cups and silver goblets sparkle with the reflection of hydrangeas.*

RIGHT: *This outdoor dining room sits amid a green oasis near downtown Dallas. The built-in banquette and broken-tile-topped table seat twelve. Balustrade urns form a window overlooking other nooks in the garden. Casual dinnerware and bright colors give it a festive feel.*

the South, and our taste for nature is reflected in the organic elements found throughout our rooms. A classical urn teeming with seashells, a haphazard spray of bean pods in a dented pewter pitcher, twigs and berries and pomegranates assembled on the tabletop. These unexpected combinations suggest a fascination with simple yet sophisticated beauty. Multitudes of windows are carefully draped in gossamer fabrics that let in the sunlight and flow with the breeze. French doors flung open allow the world outside to make a grand entrance.

THE OUTDOOR DINING ROOM

Southerners often take advantage of cool breezes, starry nights, and a mild spring sun by eating out-of-doors. The garden is a favorite spot for this. So too is a balcony, a porch, even a tent in a field far removed from all else. Mild climes in the South make it possible to be outdoors almost year-round, and anywhere we set a table, spread out a blanket, or fix a tray becomes a temporary dining room.

Patio dining increases the appetite, with the vitality of fresh air and ever-changing environmental stimuli, but Southerners also desire the same comfortable experience that indoor dining affords. So the climate has to be ideal, with just the right calm breeze and warm but not scalding sunshine. The view should be compelling, whether it consists of a scene featuring the pool, the pavilion, or a profusion of blooming flowers. It makes no difference. In simply escaping walls and ceilings, there is freedom, and nothing is more life affirming than nature.

Whether as elaborate as formal dining or as simple as taking tea in the garden, dining outdoors can mean many things. We may choose not to use Grandmother's china, but we'll also reject paper plates. Here, rough, coarse textures of grass, stone, and brick are often complemented by colorful, whimsical glasses or pottery, or bright mosaics with their shards of colored porcelain. Cool, crisp whites, in the form of napkins and tablecloths, help dispel the heat of a hot summer day. Just as the formal dining room can be over-the-top with drama and showpieces, the props used outdoors can explore an entirely different theme from the rest of the home's interiors. Woven baskets are, of course, right at home here, though they're more likely to hold bread or flowers than the picnic lunch.

All the elements of indoor dining can be set up to create a comfortable arrangement. Tables—round, oval, or rectangular—may rest under a covered porch or loggia. Here cane, wicker, and wood materials work together to underscore the natural feel of the setting. And when dining in the wide-open fields, wrought-iron or teak furnishings are often used, for they weather the elements exceptionally well. Add in plenty of chairs and benches, and bring out pillows, tablecloths, and napkins for an outdoor setting that rivals any found indoors. Large urns overflowing with freshly picked hydrangea blossoms look at home next to a brick wall when lush landscapes are within a couple of feet.

Al fresco dining implies a communion with nature in all its decadence. And a certain restrained decadence is a trait that Southerners cultivate. For in the South, where the landscape spreads out lush and green, where kudzu creeps over trees, fences, and signposts, fancy, elegant dining areas are really just an extension of the environment. In the end, what diners really want is simply to be fed—to take in the inspired surroundings, the creative approaches, the conversation, and the camaraderie.

ABOVE: *Etched glass and blue-and-white china sparkle with loose bouquets of handpicked flowers.*

OPPOSITE: *A quiet escape, the rustic loggia is furnished with a Florentine candle-burning chandelier and primitive pieces found in San Miguel, Mexico.*

PREVIOUS PAGE: *Though the temperatures may reach into the hundreds in Pass Christian, Mississippi, this dining spot offers a cool respite for taking tea or simply enjoying the nearby live oaks while rocking on the porch.*

CHAPTER III

Sleeping
Areas

Now she lay in one of the big white-painted iron sleeping-porch beds with the mosquito net folded back against its head; it was like a big baby buggy that, too, would carry her somewhere against her will. . . . Outside the summer day shimmered and rustled, and the porch seemed to flow with light and shadow that traveled outwards.

—Eudora Welty, *Delta Wedding*

ABOVE: *A Louis XVI chair, a Louis XV commode, and an antique trumeau mirror may belong in a French château, but the choice of wall covering—an updated toile de Jouy—the painted bedstead, and the painted floor bring the whole arrangement into the late twentieth century.*

OPPOSITE: *This master bedroom is rich with subtle patterns—in the wall covering, the antique rug, the mirror frame, the chaise upholstery, and even the wood's patina.*

MANY SOUTHERNERS REMEMBER LIFE BEFORE AIR-CONDITIONING, when hot, humid summer nights were relieved by natural, cooling cross-breezes. While no one today can resist the pleasures of artificial climatization, we still long for the openness of the sleeping porch or a high-ceilinged room filled with windows that let in the morning light and an evening moon.

In the last century and the early years of this one, pure bed linens that breathed deeply and dried quickly were necessities because of the heat. Despite the conveniences of poly-cotton blends today, Southerners still opt for the nostalgia and comfort of high thread counts, a characteristic of Egyptian cotton and other pure woven textiles. The fabrics that dress the bedstead block out light when necessary. When open, they shape the view.

Then there's the stereotype that the image of Scarlett O'Hara refuses to let us escape—of romance and high drama, of trousseaus and long honeymoons. New Orleans, Savannah, and Charleston probably best represent that romantic view of the South. Civilized, chivalric societies on the surface, these cities are also hotbeds of style and eccentricity, not to mention sex appeal. Bedrooms can look like stage sets, with dressmaker details on

75

bedsteads, soaring ceilings, and rich colors to equal the ardor of passionate love scenes played out in Southern works of fiction such as Tennessee Williams's *A Streetcar Named Desire* or Margaret Mitchell's *Gone with the Wind*.

The bedroom is larger now than it has been in the recent past. Not just a place for sleep and romance, it's also become a place to take care of everyday business in a relaxing ambience. Desks and chairs, tables and cabinets, have entered the domain once reserved for mattresses and box springs. Southerners are also returning to the dressing room, taking to heart the "I'm worth it" attitude of today and embracing the amenities of luxury—vanity tables, daybeds, slipper chairs, and antique Venetian mirrors.

Similarly, guest quarters are adorned to indulge and pamper. Unlike the larger and lighter master bedroom, these rooms are smaller, and they are often filled with pattern and color. Here, special touches welcome friends and family—books of verse, antique linens, porcelain vases filled with fresh stems.

Regardless of the area chosen for sleep or respite, we realize that our ancestors—who might pass their days gathered around the warm fire or tea table in a single bedchamber—had it right all along. The bedroom is the place to be.

THE MASTER BEDROOM

This Atlanta bedroom was clearly created for relaxation as well as sleep. With three seating areas, a fireplace, and family photographs scattered throughout, the room seems designed to clear the mind, no matter the time of day.

Maybe it's the agrarian, early-rising nature of the Old South or maybe it's just that we're a region of morning people, but you will be hard-pressed to find a master bedroom that is not designed to take full advantage of sunlight, especially in the morning. Fabrics in all variations of white, from crisp linens to translucent sheers to opaque ecrus, welcome the sun when available and convey a sense of daylight when it's hidden. Traditional in taste or contemporary in feel, light and often monochromatic colors dominate.

Today there is also new appreciation for natural and painted wood. While a homeowner one hundred years ago would have heavily draped a handcrafted bedstead, his descendants will let the patina of the wood stand alone, worn in spots where hands have held, nicked in others from room-

rearranging. That distressed look, which evokes the comfort of a favorite old T-shirt or blanket, has become so desirable that contemporary furniture manufacturers are creating wear artificially, designing instant antiques to please customers who demand the history implied in worn objects, with all the conveniences of new construction.

Linens are no different. Cottons look like aged linen, matelassé coverlets resemble Grandmother's heirlooms, and quilts are replicas of relics from a farmer's attic. Both old and new counterpanes appear antique, allowing all the elements of the bedroom to work together, instilling a feeling of history, and reflecting a long heritage—true or bought—of collecting and caring.

Traditionally, most Southerners slipcovered their bedroom furniture in the summer and draped sheer cotton netting or gauze from the ceiling to protect beds from yellow-fever-infected mosquitoes that flew in through open,

unscreened windows. The loosely dressed furnishings were thus shielded from the dust and dirt that sneaked in with the bugs. Mahogany legs and arms were left exposed, however, which created a stylish, stark contrast with the cotton muslin covers. Today, summer-dressed furniture has caught on across the country, transcending regional and seasonal boundaries.

In fact, slipcovers convey a casual attitude that seems to be a defining characteristic of our time. Unlike the slipcovers of the Old South, they remain in view long past August and are used year-round. With white and off-white bed dressing, in silk and cotton duck, the white slipcovered look that worked wonders in our bedrooms now adorns the entire house.

When color does take center stage in the bedroom, it is usually with saturated shades that evoke the drama of the past. Color-rich velvet, silk, and brocade were exorbitantly expensive one hundred years ago. In fact, in the Old South, the bedstead was probably the most costly acquisition a homeowner might make. And fabrics, even if they were cotton, cost a pretty penny. The services of the upholsterer added to the tally. And finally the cost of the sheets and counterpanes that made the bed habitable put the price tag beyond that of any other piece of furniture in the house.

Today good fabrics are still expensive, yet worth it. After all, they inject a little sex appeal, and a lot of luxury, into a room. Think of Manet's famous

OPPOSITE: *Silk bed hangings suggest elegant yet restrained window treatments in this Mississippi bedroom. Floral decoration on an antique painted headboard is echoed in the bed's faded coverlet.*

RIGHT: *Linen window treatments frame views of a distant meadow, while a floor-to-ceiling sheer fabric behind the bed focuses attention forward. It serves as both a headboard and a room divider, separating the sleeping and sitting areas from the dressing room and master bathroom.*

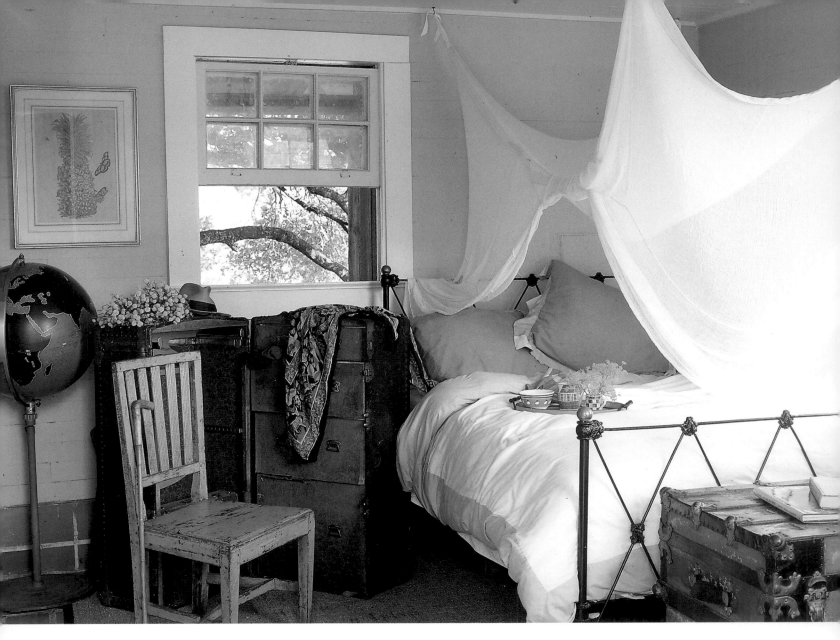

ABOVE: *An old Louisiana barn is the site for a guest bedroom where raindrops drum out a soothing beat on the tin roof during a storm. The trunk, a family heirloom, stores clothing.*

RIGHT: *A derelict table and chair become upstanding when grouped with a little highbrow Southern literature in this Pass Christian, Mississippi, bedroom. Helpless against the wear and tear of the elements, Gulf Coast cities seem to share the philosophy that distressed is best.*

RIGHT: *The term "sofa bed" takes on new meaning when the back of an antique French settee in Charlottesville, Virginia, becomes a headboard in a guest bedroom. White linens provide an inviting contrast to old cane on the settee.*

BELOW: *Inexpensive theatrical scrim filters light through the master bedroom windows. Wooden candlesticks from a Mexican church flank the iron canopy bed.*

RIGHT: *With a heavily draped bed and windows, antique furnishings, monogrammed cushions, an antique miniature portrait, and attention to the minutiae of comfort and elegance, this bedroom celebrates traditional style.*

OPPOSITE: *Dressmaker details dress up this Dallas bedroom, where rich red walls bring out the cerise hues in the draping fabric and the pillow embroidery. The decor is consistent with the eighteenth century, when bedrooms were covered head to toe with a single fabric.*

1863 painting *Olympia* (created two years before the end of the Civil War). A sumptuous bed and opulent fabrics provide a meaningful backdrop to a less-than-idealized image that is also beguiling, really seductive. Instead of floating above clouds, Olympia, in all her nakedness, looks forward with frank sexuality, underscoring one function of the bedroom that has nothing to do with sleep.

From a practical perspective, lush, opaque fabrics blocked out unwelcome light. And in the nineteenth century, they protected sleeping people from cold drafts during chilly nights. Antiques dealer and Louisiana cultural authority Robert Smith says, "The curtains would be wool and drawable, so that you could virtually make a tent out of the bed." Textiles provide the same services these days, but the real appeal is in their inherent drama, in their evocation of the past. Ruffled, swagged, and swooped fabrics that once seemed most appropriate to a grand Southern estate may turn up in a modest Baltimore cottage. Extravagant displays no longer suggest wealth. A discerning homeowner of the 1990s attends to the architecture, be it modest or grand, without letting it dictate the interior decoration, especially in the bedroom.

There does seem to be a renewed desire to return to the styles and customs of a century ago, particularly as the country becomes more and more homogenized. For many of us in the South who never let tradition go, doors are now opened wide to show the rest of the world how it's done. As with a

A very old wall panel presides over the bed in the guest room. Naive Spanish Colonial objets d'art mingle with Continental furniture to give the composition an utterly cosmopolitan feel. The king-sized bed assures a guest of the same comfort as her host.

sitting room, traditional bedrooms today can reflect a multitude of styles. For example, while many bed dressings are spare, there are plenty that are done with a canopy, a corona (*couronne* in French), or some variation. The corona, which hangs from a central crown near the ceiling and does not cover the whole surface of the bed, conveys a sense of copious fabric and elegance without weighing on the room. It becomes a sort of window treatment, or trompe l'oeil wall, that emphasizes the "over-the-top" nature of the decoration. Done well, the look is anything but, because balancing the ornate fabric treatments are Federal or Directoire antiques whose dark wood and sober design take the frills out of a fancy room.

Lest we overromanticize the past, Robert Smith reminds us that "the canopy beds usually were placed in front of windows to take advantage of the breezes. But I have a real doubt about the idyllic bucolic life, with the doors and windows thrown open and the breezes blowing through—and the bugs and animals having free run of the house."

Bedsteads have taken on a new role in the last twenty years. They hearken back to the styles of our ancestors but reflect a more cosmopolitan, contemporary aesthetic. While we have a lasting affection for the structure of a

*The curtains that sur-
round the bed in this
master bedroom close
at night to create a cocoon
beside the corner fire-
place. Amidst the naive
Mexican religious artifacts
that fill the room is an
old French fauteuil with
needlepoint upholstery.*

bed frame, the trappings can be constricting. Many of us prefer to use a relic
from the Old South and give it a new role in the bedroom. The headboard,
whether it's a sturdy wrought-iron gate, the caned back of an antique French
settee, a wall panel, or an old carved door, evokes a time and place without the
pitfalls of a rickety antique. To finish off the look, upholstered benches, side
tables, or an ottoman will rest at the foot of the mattress, providing another
surface to stack books and magazines and still suggest a complete bedstead.

Such attention reflects a personal interest in a space that was formerly
overlooked. But the master bedroom gives as much pleasure to its owner as
the living room. No wonder designers are now focusing equal attention on
both spaces.

SEATING AREAS

The color of gray flannel suiting, this Maryland master bedroom comes to life with the addition of a red tufted chaise longue.

Since French and English influences are so directly translated into Southern culture, it makes sense that we would take their customs to heart—or to bed, as the case may be. It is said that Henry VIII and Elizabeth I held audiences in their bedchambers. And the Sun King, Louis XIV, first entered the world before a crowd of witnesses who were there to attest that the new heir apparent was not an imposter. Later, he received his courtiers in his bedchamber. Marcel Proust did the same with his guests.

ABOVE: *Needlepoint pillows top chairs that are pulled up to a simple gaming table. An ideal spot to play chess or cards while enjoying tea, the space before the window is enhanced by the view.*

RIGHT: *An antique chinoiserie sewing table holds a collection of ceramics that includes a rather bold lamp, a scenic English vase, and petite porcelain boxes. The colors on the porcelain and the motifs on the table are repeated in the fabric that covers the armchair.*

Literature tells of our illustrious forebears taking often to their beds with real or imagined maladies. Considering how much time was spent recuperating in bedrooms, they were built to accommodate chairs for visitors and tables for silver trays piled high with food.

Our need for recuperative space may have diminished—thanks to advances in modern medicine and a healthy dose of modesty—but large, living room–sized bedrooms have gained in popularity. While the office, with its impersonal e-mails and the Internet, remains the principal place for business, the bedchamber has become a space to undertake personal matters of a more civilized sort, such as writing invitations or thank-you notes, journal writing, and reading.

If there is one piece of furniture other than the bed in the room, it will be a comfortable, stylish chair that does double duty as a seat of repose and glorified valet. The tradition for bedroom seating goes back at least one hundred years, when the wing chair, what our ancestors called an easy chair, was de rigueur in the most stylish bedrooms. In fact, it rarely showed up in grand Southern sitting rooms. According to Liza Gusler, curator of education at Colonial Williamsburg in Virginia, "A chamber pot was stored under the cushion, so the homeowner didn't have to go outside if the need arose."

A small writing desk does double duty as a night table and a work surface. The serene painting sets the mood for the contemporary space.

An all-white bedroom in Houston celebrates the idea of contrasts within a single color palette. The modest room looks grand because of the monochromatic walls and the abundant light. Antique sconces illuminate bedtime reading material as well as the owner's portrait of Rita Hayworth.

Similarly, bedrooms might have a set of six chairs, rather than the twelve that would fill a parlor. "A lady might have tea in her bedroom, or she would do needlework with friends. And remember, there might be only two fires going during the day—one of which was in the bedroom, probably the warmest place in the main house," says Gusler.

Luckily, we no longer live with the same sorts of hardships. And while we would rarely have use for six chairs in a bedroom, two may still be welcome to surround a table laden with tea stuffs, an afternoon indulgence borrowed from the English. Of course, the tea may be replaced by exotic liqueurs in the evening, as the chairs come together before a tall, dramatic hearth. (The fact that our climate makes a fireplace all but useless in some areas has never been of consequence. The pleasures of a roaring fire are timeless and make our current affinity for air-conditioning that much dearer.)

Underscoring our appreciation for romance in the bedroom is the presence of chaise longues. In years past we had the luxury of relatively quiet,

A Montgomery guest room is filled with carved-fruitwood twin canopy beds from the Far East that rest atop masonry floors. Both beds are served by one long table, while richly detailed bedspreads and linens soften the monastic feel of the room.

TV-less nights, where relaxing in a diaphanous negligee was commonplace—at least in theory. The chaise longue, France's supremely indulgent chair, was and continues to be the ultimate prop, and we have adopted it as our own. It is languid and elegant, as much about looking good as being infinitely comfortable, and its upholstery, whether simple or sublime, holds the promise of relaxation.

Furniture like chaise longues and daybeds could transform the central passage or entry into yet another sleeping area. In states like Virginia, "the central passage would almost always be furnished with a couch—what we call a daybed—and a set of chairs," says Gusler. "The upstairs rooms might be constructed two rooms deep, so cross-ventilation did not exist. On a hot night, you could come downstairs and sleep in comfort, or nap in the afternoon. It was one of the most comfortable rooms in the house," she says. The daybed is still an important part of the Southern interior, and it shows up in guest rooms, large master bedrooms, and even family rooms and studies.

ABOVE: *Shutters direct light across an Empire daybed in a diminutive guest room. An earthy green color gives the space color and warmth.*

RIGHT: *In a Virginia guesthouse, a stone floor serves as a backdrop for a French* duchesse, *an adaptation of a chaise longue. A swagged window treatment creates a decorative frame without blocking the view of the countryside. The "blinds" are actually one single striped shade.*

THE GUEST BEDROOM

In our mobile society, most of us travel enough to be accustomed to and appreciative of the standard comforts provided by a good hotel room. In addition to such comforts, the most successful hotels offer a bit of the charm and hospitality that we're used to at home. For guests, careful hosts combine the best of both worlds: the standard comfort and autonomy of an excellent hotel room and the welcoming feel of the familiar.

Hospitality has always been one of the bedrocks of Southern culture. As a result, an extraordinary amount of attention and detail go into the guest bedroom. After all, the visitor is away from home, and every effort is made to provide for all concerns, all possible comforts, and all desires. "Historically," says Gusler, "wealthy families have always kept nicely furnished rooms for guests. They had balls and parties that lasted for days, so they had to provide some accommodations. There are accounts of girls of

This antique spindle bed takes up residence in the master bedroom. Simple drawings and prints stand out against the patterned wall covering. An old French quilt atop the bed speaks of years of care and use.

the family sleeping in one room, while the boys of the family slept in an out-building—the schoolhouse—to make room for all the guests."

With that spirit in mind—hospitality above all else—contemporary hosts will make certain that closets have blankets and extra pillows, in addition to a handy heirloom throw draped across the foot of the bed and decorative and supportive cushions strewn around the room. Mirrors will be clear; lighting, flattering; flowers, fresh; water, bottled; and the books, an equal measure of fluff and stuff.

No matter how petite the room, a table and chair will provide a surface for working and late-night snacks. Further, you will rarely encounter the same sort of monochromatic scene that exists in the master bedroom. Who is willing to risk invading a guest's private space with light window shades and bright morning sun when all he wants is a cold compress and a hot cup of coffee? Cozy, comforting, secure are more in line with the types of adjectives that describe contemporary guest chambers.

The rooms also present a few opportunities for hosts: to decorate a room according to personal taste without having to live with those choices on a daily basis, and to make the most of small, sometimes oddly configured spaces. When a bedroom is covered in printed fabric, the boundaries of the room seem to disappear, making it seem larger and its edges softer than paint or even wallpaper might. Toile de Jouy, the eighteenth-century cartoon-filled textile, is particularly popular today and has found renewed purpose in guest rooms on the cusp of the twenty-first century. By enveloping the rooms and

This West Palm Beach master bedroom includes a chaise longue, a diminutive desk that doubles as a vanity, a chair, a sisal rug covered with kilims, and an old bedstead— all aspects of an up-to-date Southern bedroom. But this bamboo version of a bedstead has an exotic look that is entirely appropriate to the tropical climate.

furnishings in the patterns and colors of times past, contemporary hosts evoke the feeling of that bygone era and all the hospitality therein. At the same time, the fabrics' bucolic motifs, filled with idyllic scenes of farm and garden life, once again refer to the environment, to the surrounding landscape that is so important to a Southern interior, whether the property is in an urban or rural setting.

Antique accommodations, such as a tall, antique four-poster bed, or, even better, antique campaign beds or wrought-iron frames from France, Italy, or Sweden, frequently show up in the guest bedroom. The frame of choice is usually a pair of twin beds because they can accommodate a single guest or two. While it is rare to see a truly antique bed in the master bedroom—few survived the Civil War and fewer still are in decent condition because of the passage of time and the destructive nature of our climate—the guest room is usually the place to showcase whatever prized pieces still exist.

In fact, the master bedroom has become the site for the king- or queen-sized bed, where comfort and convenience on a daily basis are of utmost importance. Other, smaller antique frames, which may be twin or full-sized or even more irregular, almost always end up in the guest room. There, charming, handcrafted old beds that are always comfortable for a short stay are flanked by delicate antique side tables keeping company with collections of precious porcelains and diminutive boxes or perfume bottles.

While most guest rooms represent a departure from the master bedroom, there are some that seem like modified versions of their grander counterparts. Since imitation is the sincerest form of flattery, a guest room that duplicates the master bedroom suggests the host wants the same for her guest that she provides for herself.

Those guest rooms that contrast strongly with the master bedroom become sanctuaries, as much for the homeowner as the guest. Such a room will reflect all the care and attention that goes into a special retreat. In it, any guest is sure to feel as welcome as a member of the family—for an appropriate length of time, of course.

CHAPTER IV

Accessories

The old portraits on the walls had been dignified and gracious and had looked down upon guests with an air of mellowed hospitality.

—Margaret Mitchell, *Gone with the Wind*

WHILE INTERIORS MAY BE DOMINATED BY FURNITURE, accessories transform spaces into individual expressions of taste. The room proportions may be perfect, the sofas and chairs—whether a selection of treasured heirlooms or newly minted pieces—may be well chosen, the rugs may be lavishly Oriental or cool natural weaves, but it's in the room's details that personal style truly comes alive. The goal is simple—to make a house or apartment a home and to tell a story about the inhabitants.

The narrative threads of each room's story may be a treasured collection of botanical prints, a grouping of ever-popular blue-and-white Canton china, or a series of floral arrangements from the family garden. Delightful vignettes of heirloom photographs, artwork, porcelains, and flowers fill surfaces that reveal much about the intimate details of our lives and loves. Memories spill forth from the Southern attic and find their way into these vignettes—a piece or two of grandmother's silver, a carefully preserved bit of lace, even newspaper clippings artfully framed.

How objects are combined and arranged is as telling as what is chosen to be displayed. An accent of needed color, whether to complement highly saturated shades or to punch up a neutral background, is often a primary goal. A loose arrangement of red tulips (even in winter) or a tightly clumped spray of lavender in a silver cup will brighten any corner or season.

ABOVE: *Contrasting a punch of pale pink roses with a robust piece of clay pottery highlights the idea that formal and informal elements can coexist.*

OPPOSITE: *A contemporary take on sporting art shows up in a Paris apartment, where a series of horse heads and a sculpture preside over a chest of drawers covered in 1920s wallpaper.*

A gathering of palm fronds in an umbrella stand may bring spring to an entry that is otherwise dulled by the grayness of winter.

Rooms brim with stories: a bookshelf filled with a lifetime's collection; artwork hung carefully to be savored by appreciative guests; botanical elements chosen to welcome the outdoors in. It is, as is often said, all in the details.

ARTWORK

Few elements in the home reflect more personality and recall more memories than the art that hangs on its walls. But art is a relatively new idea in the South. The lack of large metropolitan areas in Southern states and the strong influence of Protestantism in the eighteenth and early nineteenth centuries kept the general public from exposure to the same work that filled museums and churches elsewhere. Purity of space and sparseness of decor were defining elements. And for a long time, art created in the South was overlooked. John Singer Sargent and later Andy Warhol were America's claim to art fame. But in the last twenty years, whole museums devoted to Southern art have been built, not to celebrate Southern art above works created in other areas of the country, but to reveal the great store of talent that was so long overlooked. And the major cities of the South—Atlanta, New Orleans, Houston, Miami—have become centers of regional art production, where galleries represent local artists with international reputations.

Eighteenth-century Southern art began, naturally, with portraits, landscapes, and sporting art—hunting and fishing scenes—which exemplified the cultural importance of family and a historic connection to the land. Later, photography became an equally important art form. In the eighteenth century, as the South became increasingly prosperous, gentlemen and ladies of means were painted by artists known for their portrait work. But there were also itinerant portrait artists who carried around naive painted torsos and then added the faces that distinguished each subject. These works were rarely signed, and there is usually no indication as to the identity of the sitter. Now these paintings show up throughout Southern interiors, introducing visitors to a long-dead relative or even to a purchased portrait, an "instant ancestor" of unknown origin, who may bear a faint resemblance to the family and who can be claimed, tongue in cheek, as a blood relation.

Similarly, cut silhouettes that were mostly created in the nineteenth century underscore the sense of history that a Southern house seems to convey. While the subject's past may be a mystery, the hints of identity—a collar,

ABOVE: *White roses stand pure and ageless atop a contemporary handcrafted console with finials bearing the marks of time.*

OPPOSITE: *Often we are reluctant to hang art on patterned walls for fear they might clash or get lost within each other. The subject of this antique panel appears to be inspired by images in the surrounding toile wall covering.*

The botanical prints in a New Orleans home are hung in much the same way our ancestors might have presented them. An S-shaped hook, suspended from the ceiling molding, holds the wires and supports the art, saving the walls from damage and nail holes.

spectacles, hairstyle—indicate his or her age and the date of the piece, making the work a portrait of the most subtle sort.

Landscape paintings are another form of art that frequently appears in Southern interiors. Antique examples may be inherited, but they are prized, and often purchased today for their documentation of a place before development and urban sprawl obscured the landscape that our ancestors settled and farmed. Contemporary works capture those areas that are still pure and untouched and also portray what urbanization has done to the Southern landscape. Further, they emphasize the idea that interiors draw inspiration

from their exteriors; landscape paintings, more than any other genre, celebrate nature.

Animal paintings, whether depicting sport or farm life, are reappearing on our walls. A mostly English genre, this style of painting crossed the Atlantic in the eighteenth century and captivated the Southern landed gentry. Paintings may depict prized horses, cows for sale, or a particularly porky pig. The formality of the composition and the informality of the subject seem the perfect juxtaposition in contemporary interiors, where fine furniture is as comfortable as it is pedigreed.

Industrialism and the emergence of larger Southern cities stimulated population growth and cultural education, which prompted an appreciation for art and strengthened its role in the home. Today, while tastes for old favorites die hard, interiors are filled with works that range in period and style from the Old Masters to new forms of abstract expressionism.

Of the more traditional sort, prints that are actually plates taken from eighteenth- and nineteenth-century pattern books often appear in groups on walls and above sofas, ascending and descending staircases, and tucked into corners of bedrooms, bathrooms, and kitchens. They depict anything from

images of French rulers to hand-colored botanical and zoological studies and patterns from ceramics factories. Hand-colored versions and color lithographs tend to be the most popular because of the ornamentation they lend to a vignette, but original black-and-white versions, with their detailed drawings, can be particularly dramatic, especially when hung on a patterned or colored wall.

Abstract art has introduced a new vocabulary into interiors previously dominated by form and structure, where color conveys a landscape, seemingly haphazardly drawn lines suggest a portrait, and amorphous objects transmit a message. With our emphasis on comfort and unpretentiousness, abstract art frees us from the strictures of tradition and injects a level of unpredictability and timeliness into interiors. In fact, the careful play of traditional or antique with contemporary elements is what gives an interior its interest. Traditional works, such as botanical prints and landscapes, may

Hanging large works of art above doorways and windows raises the eye and makes this small living room feel grand.

A painting by Utah artist Bruce Brainard hangs above a contemporary mantel. This space encompasses all the serenity conveyed in the painting with all the classical style of good contemporary design.

adorn a room filled with modern overstuffed sofas and sisal rugs. Contemporary mixed-media pieces are displayed amid seventeenth-century tables and antique silver tea sets. Although Southerners of the New South are willing to break with tradition when we decorate, we require that art work with its surroundings. That's not to say that we buy art to match the sofa. It's to say that an important painting, rather than a sofa, may dictate, or at least influence, a room's color scheme and layout.

Of course, there are a few challenges inherent in combining old and new, representational and abstract, particularly when large spaces have to be accommodated. Grand antique works are hard to come by and expensive. So Southerners have become incredibly resourceful when grouping smaller old paintings or prints that can be read as one large work of art. By coordinating frames and mats around similarly themed subjects, and hanging several in a vertical or horizontal grid, the required space is filled; the space is made to

RIGHT: *Southern regional style even makes it across the Atlantic, to Paris, where a portrait presides over a color-rich vignette that includes small green viburnum blossoms and black-and-white photographs of the owner's parents.*

OPPOSITE: *Often art balances other furnishings and accessories. This brightly painted chest is utterly appropriate to Baltimore, considering the city's heritage of decorative painting. It could easily be too much for the room, but with the mixed media work above echoing the color, the other pieces and fabric are successfully brought into the vignette.*

look inviting. If a group of images looks stark, Southerners often resort to the centuries-old method of using S-shaped hooks to grip ceiling moldings and hold wire that suspends prints and paintings in front of a wall. Crisscrossing ribbon, rope, or wire transforms a practical necessity into a decorative motif that literally ties together the individual works.

Color, too, can be used to unify disparate works. When prints are hung on a colored or patterned wall, the wall acts as one large mat and transforms them into a whole arrangement. In the eighteenth and nineteenth centuries, paint, hand-painted wallpaper, and fabric were costly and thus signified wealth. Early Southerners would not have changed a wall color to white to give a painting a neutral backdrop, nor would they have sacrificed wallpaper to prevent a visual clash with a work of art. To their eyes, bold color enhanced any room, and wallpaper, with or without a painting hung over it, was a work of art in itself. A floral, stripe, damask, or textured fabric background in a bedroom or sitting room gives a surprising lift to a piece of art,

Distressed Greek, Roman, and Etruscan artifacts bring out the colors of the drawing by nineteenth-century French artist Georges Goursat, also known as Sem. The vignette adeptly combines two vastly different cultures: classical antiquity and the Beaux Arts.

as long as the image remains the single clearly representational picture on the wall.

Large-scale contemporary art may be easier to come by, but it can also overpower a space. In that instance, it's important to consider the subject and the color palette. With traditional English or French furniture, strongly abstract works can be compelling, as long as they reflect the same classic principles that inspired the antiques. A neutral room calls for a work that is similarly muted but perhaps more representational, since its monochromatic palette can blur the lines that distinguish each piece of furniture.

When a favorite piece is too small for a desired wall and too important to share space with other art or accessories, altering the size of the frame works wonders. Placing the art in a large mat and bold frame gives added depth and significance to the subject. The new size can correct the proportions of the work and fill the needed space.

Bookshelves are obvious repositories for classic Southern literature, but they are also clever backdrops for small paintings, prints, and wonderful old photographs. Perching a small photograph on an easel presents it as a work of art that can share space with other paintings and sculptural objects and not look out of place. In fact, easels are important tools in vignettes where placement of a painting, especially a small one, is key. If a small artwork is hung on the wall, it may be obscured by other objects. An easel helps a small photograph or oil on canvas to come forward and stand out.

And who says that wall art really must be *hung* on the wall? Paintings and prints lean just as well as they hang. Photographs, accessories, or even flowers in different sizes, shapes, and condition work together to give texture and color to a still life that sits atop a table. Leaning one piece against another pulls the objects together into one coherent image. And by constant visual editing, a hodgepodge of diverse pieces can actually be made to read as a clear, stylish display.

Living with art is just that: using paintings, prints, and photographs that sustain memories, create windows, and shape dreams.

Unexpected methods of hanging art can give it more prominence and wake up a quiet space at the same time. These paintings by Julie Bloom would look great anywhere. Hung on the shelf amid innumerable books, they take on new importance.

COLLECTIONS

Old American pottery emerges from its display space in a rustic kitchen cabinet. Although the pottery seems naive, it is a highly sought after collectible because of the unique craftsmanship that went into the creation of each vessel.

Southerners are born collectors. Many an attic below the Mason-Dixon Line holds its own micromuseum of Southern culture. Family furniture and old silver are moved about and polished with the utmost care. But treasured also are less precious remembrances: a collection of hats, family photographs, or flea market glassware. We're drawn to the shine of silver, its brilliance displayed in ornate candlesticks or worn mint julep cups. We find the simplicity of epicurean objects appealing, be they rustic jugs and jars, or plates and platters bordered in blue.

A mix of old and new pottery provides rich contrasts of form, color, and texture on a dining room sideboard.

Collections usually consist of old objects, and most valued are pieces that are handmade. European porcelain and silver, American pottery and furniture, canes, and doorknobs made before the Industrial Revolution were created with true craftsmanship. As a result, each object in a collection is individual. There may be a nick in the wood, a flaw in the painting, a scratch on the glass. The lack of perfection is endearing.

Showcasing a collection no longer means lining up objects like artifacts in a museum. Some pieces, like pottery and porcelain, may be kept handy for daily use. Others are combined in artful still-life vignettes that not only beautify a room but also illustrate the owner's personal interests, culture, and style.

Since tradition is a pervasive element of Southern culture, and nothing says South more than a silver tea or coffee set, it is fair to expect to find quite a bit of silver in a household. In Memphis, they celebrate their own unique tradition of using silver goblets instead of crystal glasses to hold wine

ABOVE: *Quirky objects such as crystal banister finials, inkwells, and globes of different sizes focus attention atop an iron writing table. Red walls and sunlight streaming in through windows bounce reflections off the glass.*

RIGHT: *A kaleidoscope of colors greets visitors who enter this New Orleans home. Light shines through a collection of eighteenth- and nineteenth-century hand-blown bottles, displayed on an antique French wine bottle tree.*

BELOW: *Old hats and walking sticks lean and hang on a hat rack in the entry hall. Once useful objects, the hats and sticks are now showcased as works of art.*

RIGHT: *Sometimes collections can be found in their entirety, like these old shoes purchased at one location and then stacked on an eighteenth-century staircase model.*

and spirits. Inherited, bought, or borrowed, English and American antique silver takes a place of honor in Southern homes.

A precious metal regarded as second only to gold since very early times, silver has always received special attention and care. Those centuries-old objects have endured hardship, neglect, and general wear—just like our ancestors. Today, cabinets and armoires full of silver tureens, tea caddies, coffeepots, and flatware get rather protective treatment—regular polishing, felt blankets that prevent tarnishing, and safe storage.

Fortunately, even if silver has not been zealously cared for, it retains its appeal, aesthetically and historically. While much silver still sparkles like new, some collectors have discovered an alternative to polishing in this era of twelve-hour workdays. With our newfound appreciation for the patina of age and use, slightly tarnished silver, with its coppery glow, is considered quite attractive and has become the innovative, inadvertent accessory of the turn of this century.

Southerners will always place silver serving sets atop old sideboards, the same way our English ancestors did. But to mix things up a bit, the teapot may become a vase for a bouquet of flowers. Or a silver set placed on a fabric-covered ottoman will make the silver seem less precious—and the ottoman more so. Antique mint julep cups or old silver creamers at each place setting on a table give individual guests a personal flower arrangement. And no bit of silver conveys as much drama as an antique candelabra whose silver decoration is as thick with relief molding as the wax gathered on the bobeches at the bases of the candles.

Our passion for silver is almost equaled by our love of ceramics— antique French Sèvres and English Wedgwood; rustic New England and Southern pottery; and Imari from Japan or blue-and-white or rose medallion from China. Tables are set; sideboards and buffets, filled to the brim; walls, adorned; bathrooms, marked; and bedrooms, sedated with personal collections that speak of taste, travels, and exotic dreams. No space is immune as we mix old and new, refined and rustic.

One of the most exciting ways to treat ceramics is also most unexpected. Take them out of the dining room. Hung on a wall in a grid, plates and platters present a front similar to antique prints. Atop a mantel, they support a larger work, such as a mirror or painting. And on a side table, they inject a shot of color and form into a space normally cluttered with keys, coasters, and books. Placement atop a small stack of books can give a plate height. A colored wall will help their patterns sing. No matter what, put

A row of antique baskets fill blank wall space between the cherry armoire and the ceiling. Their worn patina echoes the natural tones of the wood and emphasizes the point that this Louisiana home is one that is deeply rooted in the environment—and the past.

them in a place where they cannot be dislodged and broken. For Southern style is not about making friends and family ill at ease, afraid to touch, lest they break a treasured piece. It's about a perception of comfort that is as real as the furniture.

Sometimes an arrangement that pairs fine and not-so-fine objects works to highlight an important collection. For example, a shot of color, even if it comes from something as mundane as a collection of old *National Geographic* magazines, can make neighboring collectibles like Mexican ceramics seem much more important. The clean, simple stacks with their brilliant yellow spines juxtaposed with terra-cotta-colored pottery statues and standing plates help the bookshelves shed their staid literary image. The combination of colors and shapes enlivens shelves and transforms ubiquitous objects into extraordinary decorative elements.

Mounted on the wall, the collection of wooden pond yachts is readily seen but safely out of harm's way. Too old and worn to perform on the water, the yachts cover one family room wall.

Mexican ceramics and National Geographic magazines rescued from the attic serve as striking complements to each other arranged in a bookcase. The terra-cotta color of the ceramics juxtaposed with the yellow spines of the magazines makes the all-white backdrop come to life.

The characters created by some of the South's greatest writers, such as William Faulkner and Flannery O'Connor, paint an image of the region that occasionally exposes the darkest sides of its culture. But they also insightfully portray an eccentricity that is unlike any other in the country. Blame it on the heat, the history, whatever seems reasonable, but Southerners have come to wear their quirkiness like a badge of honor.

Collections reflect that eccentricity, particularly when antique dress forms come together in a bedroom corner, old shoes walk up an antique model staircase, and old combs fan across a dressing table. Lives that have gone before stay with us in the most intimate relics of the past. Stacks of old hats and hat-making forms that were once stored in a trunk now hang on hat racks next to old walking sticks and umbrellas, giving the illusion of a houseful of nineteenth-century guests. Nautical tributes like barometers, pond yachts, and black-and-white regatta photographs placed among land-

ABOVE: *Natural accessories like these shells and corals piled in a classical-style urn recall trips to the seashore. They also create a compelling organic contrast with the vessel that holds them.*

RIGHT: *A wild floral arrangement combining sticks, leaves, and tulips gives a natural feel to the mantel. The bright blue bird sculpture injects a bit of whimsy, inviting a closer look at everything around it.*

OPPOSITE: *A simple mirror serves as a backdrop to museum-quality blue-and-white porcelain whose floral arrangements—blue delphiniums and blue and white hydrangeas—make their colors seem more intense.*

locked accessories, such as polished rocks, make dynamic objects sit still while inanimate objects tell a story.

To add some texture and a hint of nature, rustic baskets can serve as receptacles for fruit and vegetables in the kitchen, or they can fill blank space atop an armoire in a living room or bedroom. Woven straw baskets make a room seem casual, approachable, because of their functional origins.

FLOWERS

Of course, no home is complete without the ultimate accessory of nature, the fresh arrangement. They have no function other than a sensory one, but live, natural arrangements are as necessary as water to a region so closely tied to its surroundings. Sultry summers help cutting gardens flourish. Fresh-cut flowers, when brought inside, bring a little cool color to the steamiest August afternoon.

ABOVE: *The traditional red rose is always a safe bet to contribute color in a vignette. For a touch of formality on a tabletop, a small, tight bunch of red roses creates a contrast that highlights the beauty of the fine china and silver.*

RIGHT: *Contemporary silver comes together for afternoon tea. The silver tray that holds the creamer and sugar bowl is actually a fine silver picture frame, and the vase that holds the bouquet of lilies is a champagne flute.*

OPPOSITE: *Orchids are particularly useful when an accessory with height and color is needed. A fine ceramic cachepot reflects the care required to propagate the fickle flower.*

It's tempting to bring out the crystal vase when decorating with roses or tulips, but it's more fun to introduce new containers for a different look. Although roses present a challenge for the gardener, a cluster of the porcelain-like blossoms can make a humble vessel look pristine or a refined vase positively exquisite. Many Southerners collect pottery made from the region's clay-rich soil and use it to hold fresh stems. A container filled with a loose arrangement of cuttings puts a special piece in perspective, as a vessel to be admired certainly, but also to be used.

Another unexpected choice to hold flowers might be a champagne flute. What a surprise for dinner guests to see such fresh and unexpected arrangements at their place settings. We typically use round vessels for flowers, but different shapes challenge the everyday. And baskets filled with flowers can emphasize the natural essence of the woven vessels. Some flowers may be presented without a container at all. Stiff-stemmed calla lilies, sunflowers, or even daisies, tied with ribbon or raffia, work anywhere and give a short-lived dash of life to their audience.

ABOVE: *The exotic poppy, with its curvy, spindly stems and vibrant color, adds a bit of distinction to interiors more accustomed to roses and hydrangeas. An antique barometer gets more attention thanks to the color and form of the flower.*

RIGHT: *No space can remain quiet when sunflowers are in the picture. They splash interiors with sunshine and draw the eye to whatever artwork or accessories are nearby.*

OPPOSITE: *A basket full of delphiniums gives much-needed height to a low arrangement that includes an antique daybed. The palmettos leaning in the far corner offer a casual and surprising boost of color and form.*

When a big splash of color is needed to brighten an area, flowers from the home garden or florist serve beautifully. Blossoms of the same color family or genus may serve as accents in a small vase or as a centerpiece when gathered into a large container. Sunflowers are a particularly good choice for impact. A loose arrangement of chrysanthemums adds a seasonal touch and also jazzes up the earth tones in fabrics and furnishings. Hydrangeas, with their colors of blue and purple, white and green, are particularly popular in the months of May and June. The blossoms are abundant and accessed from profusely blooming bushes. Their balls of color make effortless, elegant arrangements. In fact, a single blue French hydrangea in a small glass jar suggests a mass of flowers because of the large, round blossoms.

Just as mantels serve as stages for art and collections, they also work for flowers. A piece of artwork on a mantel top may be flanked by fresh flower arrangements or, for a twist, partnered with just one. To prevent the

ABOVE: *Neutrals from the garden are sometimes all that is necessary to accessorize an area. These viburnums coordinate simply with a subtly patterned wall covering and delicate, blown-glass bottles.*

RIGHT: *Grasses and mosses offer a rustic alternative to flowers in a centerpiece. Here, the rich green gives a punch of color to a predominantly white room.*

OPPOSITE: *Fruit has come out of the kitchen and the dining room, and it seems to be taking up colorful residence in living rooms and even bedrooms. In this case, the polished green of stacked apples reflects the color in the Queen Anne's lace that fills an old urn.*

mantel from looking lopsided, a few pieces of differently sized ceramics or a small sculpture will even the weight of the vignette. Think also of height and mass. A petite arrangement loses its impact next to a large work of art. Tall leaves with graphic forms provide strong, supportive accompaniment to a significant piece of art. Bookshelves also provide great, unpredictable space for flowers. A small bunch of nosegays tucked into a bookshelf can inject a little color and a lot of life into rows of brown books.

With all the colors of nature to choose from, making a decision on what to place in a favorite vase can be difficult. So we occasionally rely on neutrals. Greens, whites, and ivories look clean and contemporary, utterly

suitable to today's interiors. Who can resist oakleaf hydrangeas from the backyard placed in a silver water pitcher? Or the delicate beauty of Queen Anne's lace crowded into a white urn? These subtle arrangements speak to even subtler contrasts in the surrounding space—ecru slipcovers and mahogany furniture, Venetian glass and North Carolina pottery.

Every bit of the garden comes indoors, even the lawn. Ryegrass and moss are now grown to adorn the table. A flat of grass or bit of moss placed in a ceramic urn may be served up as an eye-catching centerpiece. Tall blades of ryegrass accentuate the form and contrast with the color of a plain terracotta pot or a pristine silver biscuit box.

Particularly when the weather's extremes won't allow for color, the sculptural forms of vines and stems create artistic accents. If these types of arrangements seem too casual and lifeless, the addition of a few colored flowers make them more dynamic. But for a more formal, albeit neutral, setting, white roses are a Southern favorite. Whether they are arranged simply in one distressed vase or in a pair of fine vases, their lack of color emphasizes the perfection of the blossom and brings a bit of formality to a setting.

The combination of fresh arrangements, eclectic collectibles, and art gives a house an identity, a personality that makes it a home. Nothing tells a story like a Southern collection, whether it's fine antiques from a French flea market or shells from the beach. Each piece stirs a memory, recounts a history. Southerners cherish these reminders of struggle and survival, reminders of family that have gone before, and look forward to a future that respects the past.

ABOVE: *Few colors bring more life to blue than yellow. The roses' accent of color draws our eye to the museum-quality porcelain. The square tole containers provide yet another contrast, one of shape and texture.*

OPPOSITE: *Fresh grasses and carved wooden birds seem to have jumped out of the painting and onto the antique sideboard.*

PREVIOUS PAGE: *Nothing is more Southern than a mint julep cup. While the cups normally come out for the Kentucky Derby in May, a Dallas homeowner makes use of hers out of season—as delicate vessels to hold white roses.*

CHAPTER V

Architecture

They were pulling into State Street at Columbiana Square . . . across the street from the tall, imposing, red brick Davenport house—its two tall chimneys flanking each end of the steep roof, relieved only by three dormer windows, . . . the tasteful fanlight arched over the high, simple colonial entrance.

—Eugenia Price, *Savannah*

ABOVE: *A strong axis in this Mediterranean-inspired Dallas house runs from the arcade entrance through the house, across a pool in the rear garden, terminating in a Palladian-style pavilion.*

OPPOSITE: *In response to climate, Charleston, South Carolina, evolved what has become known as a Charleston Single House. Varied in style, they all share the narrow end fronting the street, the long side fitted with a full-length, usually two-story porch overlooking a garden.*

THE IMAGE OF THE GREAT-COLUMNED HOUSE SHIMMERING at the end of an allée of arching live oaks will always remain, for most, the quintessential expression of Southern architecture. The reasons are sound. The Greek Revival style had a long and pervasive run in a region fueled by a plantation boom up to the Civil War, and only in the South was the full-height, and often full-facade, temple-form porch dominant. Rows of white columns linked the fledgling society to more ancient cultures than England, and the stark, sober, classical forms anchored new houses in wild, Arcadian settings.

But there is another obvious element in this picture that embodies how the South has shaped its domestic building: the landscape and the climatic conditions that encompass it. House and setting lock together like a waltzing couple. The porch is built not just to impress, but to be used during a long, warm season. The house rises high to catch the breeze and surmounts the damp, dew-covered terrain. Windows are really passages between indoors and out. All is open, flowing, light.

Such grand places, isolated in a toiling agricultural world and functioning like hotels for a far-flung social network, were exceptions. But the type speaks to an ideal—the graceful house embedded in a garden—that, historically, played out at many scales and in diverse locales across the region. It continues to this day.

As in other English colonial settlements along the Atlantic, the dominant Georgian and, later, lighter Adam or Federal styles initially ruled in Virginia, Maryland, and the Carolinas, moving inland with settlers. Soon a strongly classical yet idiosyncratic style, championed and evolved by Thomas Jefferson as proper for the new nation, began to be built in the South, especially in rural Virginia. But one need only walk the bowered streets of Charleston, South Carolina, to see how distinctively the prevailing styles of houses—their narrow sides fronting the street and long sides fitted with multilevel porches or piazzas that overlook gardens—could be transformed to fit the climate and layout of a specific location or city.

In Louisiana and areas along the Gulf Coast where initial French influences were strong, a hybrid mix of domestic architecture drew on as many

Oak Alley Plantation in Louisiana represents the South's iconic architectural image, with a great house at the end of a live oak allée and the full-height columned porch wrapping front and sides, holding its own against the powerful landscape.

The modest scale of a cottage on the Mississippi Gulf Coast captures the essence of Southern style, with pleasing pro-portion, a light lift above the ground, elegantly expressed construction, and colors in dialogue with the setting.

sources as its singular cuisine. As elsewhere, imported ways of building were soon adapted to suit the climate and ways of life. St. Augustine in Florida and mission settlements in Texas represent limited Spanish influence.

Beginning about 1830 and continuing in the South until 1860, Greek Revival dominated the region, with its clean lines and use of the temple form for everything from church to bank to mansion to shotgun house (a one-story house where ostensibly a shell entering through the front door could continue the length of the house and exit out the back door without hitting any walls). Though competing Gothic Revival and Italianate styles gained more popularity farther north, the Greek Revival prevailed in the more iso-lated, rural South until the disruption of the Civil War, and continued after as an accepted vernacular. It was even the commonly accepted way to build a remote country store.

Greek Revival was the last great single style. With exposure to publica-tions and an eclectic range of plans, the postbellum South began to follow a national trend to a more diverse and rapid sequence of styles. In towns, where growth was spurred, neighborhoods reflected a mix of expression. In larger cities, whole neighborhoods of popular house types based on the peri-od when they were built produced layers of once-dominant styles that can be read like geological strata.

Even so, the generally lower population density and more loosely laid out neighborhoods and towns in the region (when compared to their

OPPOSITE: *Urban neighborhoods in the South, like New Orleans's Garden District, grew in looser patterns than elsewhere and were bowered with trees and plants. So houses in styles found elsewhere take on a certain Southern character. Such garden districts across the region have been a favorite locale for historic preservation and new urban life.*

BELOW: *Fine residential architects are presently producing a new generation of authentic period designs in many Southern cities and towns, like this understated Regency-style house by Cole & Cole in Montgomery, Alabama.*

Northern counterparts) resulted in a distinctive character. New Orleans's Garden District, where houses stand close but separated amid the exuberant embrace of trees and plants, is one of the best-known neighborhoods of its type. But across the South, every town with prosperous residents in the late nineteenth century grew a garden district, most just a short walk from Main Street. Often protected by local historic zoning, these bucolic urban enclaves can be found in Columbus, Mississippi; Columbia, South Carolina; Greenville, North Carolina; or Greeneville, Tennessee; and in literally hundreds of other towns.

EVOLUTION OF SOUTHERN ARCHITECTURE

While the majority of houses built earlier in the century were by builders or "gentleman architects" using pattern book plans or drawing upon traditional practice, the emergence of the architecture profession in the nation and in the South during the late 1800s led to a growing number of residences designed by trained architects. Though architects were concentrated in great urban centers like New York City, Philadelphia, and Chicago, certain Southern cities supported talented people who focused on residential work and whose reputations still resonate: W. L. Bottomley in Richmond, Neil Reid and Philip Trammell Shutze in Atlanta, Birdsall Briscoe and John Staub in Houston, and, in the rarefied setting of Palm Beach, Addison Mizner, John Volk, and Marion Syms Wyeth.

A side view of Melrose (1845), one of the great houses built within park-like settings in Natchez, Mississippi, illustrates the powerful organizing effect of identically sized windows and shutters marching the length of the closely set brick wall. A very deep cornice visually bridges the gap between the giant limestone Doric columns at the front (right) and the square columns bounding the shutter-walled porch at the rear.

Though some architects, like Mizner, developed a signature style, most designed across an eclectic range adapted individually to client, program, location, and whatever else might pertain. They were often also involved in selection of furnishings and development of the grounds. A highly evolved taste and sense of style reigned. By the 1920s, these and many other less well known but skilled architects produced houses still treasured in neighborhoods across the region.

Representative of this period is Shutze's career in Atlanta, which has been documented in the book *American Classicist: The Architecture of Philip Trammell Shutze,* by Elizabeth Dowling (Rizzoli, 1989). Photographs and drawings include the grand estates that the architect designed, beginning in the 1920s. The celebrated Swan House, built by Edward Inmans and preserved as a house museum, shows the architect's facility with period styles and his understanding of how the house with surrounding gardens should be conceived as a whole. His studies of the Italian originals while at the American Academy in Rome gave him solid grounding in what a villa should be.

The Great Depression interrupted Shutze's work and that of others. With the ascendance of modernism after World War II, the line that separated

For a new house at Seaside, Florida, architect Alex Gorlin used windows and French doors fitted with thirty-five pairs of shutters as an architectural tour de force. The one exposed side elevation (shown here), which has views of the Gulf of Mexico, conveys a rigorous organization not unlike that visible in the side view of Melrose (shown opposite).

regional architecture seemed almost obliterated. But by the 1950s, a renewal had begun. Starting with historic preservation in San Antonio, self-taught architect O'Neil Ford developed a regional Texas architecture for residences and other buildings. Although Texas has many styles—East Texas is an extension of the South; coastal Texas, like Galveston, continues much of the Caribbean-influenced Gulf Coast—it is central Texas, where German settlers brought the practice of building in stone, using native limestone, that most people think of as distinctively Texan. They are correct, but the prevailing perception has more to do with material than style. What has evolved since Ford is a regional style that favors stone or a stone-colored brick used in simple masses, relieved by long porches with deep overhangs, also detailed simply.

In the 1960s, from his base in Baton Rouge, A. Hays Town moved from a general modern practice to a focus on houses across Louisiana and

ABOVE & OPPOSITE:
Over the past fifty years, Baton Rouge architect Hays Town has developed a Creole style of architecture rooted in historic building practice, with many houses arranged as a series of structures that might have been built over time. Modulated outdoor spaces and a rich palette of natural materials tune his houses to climate and setting.

Mississippi, working out his own versatile Creole style of a house made up of many parts that appear to have been built over time. Based in preservation too, Richard Koch and Samuel Wilson in New Orleans designed with a seamless understanding of what made historic buildings so appealing. In the process, they invented the enchanting New Orleans courtyard, assumed now to have always been there.

In each case, the strong regional character ran counter to the dictates of modernism, with its international, antiregional bias. Except for Ford's, the work of these and other architects tapping into tradition and place was utterly ignored by the architecture press and the design profession at large. The clients came by word of mouth, and they did keep coming. Hays Town houses in the hundreds can be found across Louisiana and the Mississippi Delta. The work struck a deep chord. These architects had found their inspiration not from their peers but from the broader culture around them. They reconnected with how others had built in the same place.

The revival was certainly not of a single style, or even a bundle of styles, but of an attitude, a way of taking the best of tradition—even aspects of modernism—and shaping it to serve both a particular client and a particular setting. The attitude often begins with an individual or firm and gets passed on to others.

Such has been the case with the late Frank McCall Jr. Based in Moultrie, Georgia, he built a reputation for designing wonderful houses over an area that extended across South Georgia to Sea Island, north to Atlanta and beyond. He had worked for many years before he became widely known, but he was immersed so deeply in his region that he could advise, by telephone, on what color a church two counties away should be painted. His practice is now carried on by the McCall-Turner firm, and his example is followed by architects who apprenticed under him. The designs range from the almost plain but perfectly proportioned classical country house to a richly ornamented Italianate villa to a sedate French town house fronting a courtyard.

Early on, McCall even designed a house with exposed concrete blocks inside and out, using such a deft hand that it looks like eighteenth-century tabby (seashell concrete historically used at the coast).

The firm O'Neil Ford founded, Ford, Powell & Carson, continues to design houses across Texas, along with major commercial and institutional work. And the firm has spawned a whole generation of practices that vigorously explore an architecture based in Texas regional roots.

More recently, the challenges to modernism begun with the postmodern movement of the 1980s have helped clear the way for a growing number of architects pursuing fine, tradition-based residential design. Some honed their skills within established firms. Many found their way through work in historic preservation, wherein old buildings literally became teachers. There are significant practices that are beginning to have major influence in places like Washington, D.C., Miami, Vero Beach, Atlanta, Birmingham, Dallas, Austin, San Antonio, and New Orleans. Other firms, like McAlpine-Tankersley, based

To give a large new residence near Washington, D.C., a scale appropriate to its eighteenth-century Georgian Colonial period, architects Versaci Neumann & Partners turned the master bedroom (right) and kitchen-family room (left) into 1 ½-story wings, and made the garage/guesthouse a separate structure (far left).

in Montgomery, Alabama, or Ken Tate in Jackson, Mississippi, have established styles and reputations that are associated nationally with the region.

What are the characteristics of these tradition-based houses? How are they similar to and how are they different from historical models? To begin with, the modernist complaint that such work merely copies earlier examples misrepresents the work. In fact, the operative word that truly describes current regional architecture is "precedent." In every case, these designs are inventive and creative but at the same time deferential to deeper regional traditions. For a client desiring a house with a grand columned portico, architect Bobby McAlpine still incorporates his favored practice of putting the entrance to one side, so the principal rooms of the house can occupy center stage. North Carolina architect Milton Grenfell, in adapting an eighteenth-century Italian Baroque lodge for a new house, found that the unusual X-plan worked well to focus the rear of the house on a lake view and screen

outdoor living space from nearby houses. And at Windsor, a classically planned resort community in Florida, architects Scott Merrill, Clemens Schaub, and others are finding that the Roman house type, with rooms and masonry walls at the property line enclosing expanded versions of the-atrium, are an effective way to maximize private outdoor living spaces attuned to the benign winter climate.

Full understanding of various historical types and the proper proportions needed is essential, and since few architectural schools today offer that in their curriculum, the new traditionalists must develop their own skills by studying historical precedents. For most, a personal library of architectural books becomes a key resource. And rather than apologizing for following what others have done, these architects point proudly to the historical examples that inform their contemporary work.

THE NEW TRADITIONALISTS

Commonly shared issues among these new traditionalists include how to achieve authentic building character with contemporary building practices. Attention to detail in drawings is essential, since standard detailing used by residential contractors is not appropriate. Georgian moldings, for example, are not right for other periods. Often, boldly scaled but simply

BELOW & OPPOSITE: *For an Atlanta show house (below) designed for Southern Accents, architects Harrison Design Associates and designer John Oetgen revived Regency style with a stone-colored brick, bowed entry and portico, parapet walls to emphasize the cubic form of the central block, and, overall, an understated classical aesthetic. The porch was inspired by the historic Owens-Thomas House (opposite) in Savannah.*

profiled trim is called for. The level of craft is important, but the old line that you can't build houses like they used to is not true. Many architects find that, when challenged, the building trades take great pride in seeing a well-crafted house realized. Of course, quality costs, as it always has. The first issue for many residential architects is to reduce the overall square footage of a house, say from 10,000 to 8,500 square feet, in order to have the budget for proper detail and materials.

The matter of size also becomes important when historical models are applied to the much larger house of today. In contrast to the common practice of a deliberately inflated structural appearance seen in today's builder market—the blocky mass with soaring rooflines and a two-story arched entry suitable for a train station—the skillful traditionalist works to create a more modest architectural expression, no matter the size of the house. The

ABOVE & OPPOSITE:
*Architectural periods like
the flamboyant Baroque,
not often employed today,
can be successfully looked
to for house designs by
architects with a ground-
ing in history. A rotunda
entry for this North
Carolina house by archi-
tect Milton Grenfell ties
together four wings of the
X-plan layout with a mar-
ble floor pattern empha-
sizing its elliptical shape.*

intent is to keep the authentic scale of the past. The plans often break the
mass of a large house into a composition of smaller volumes or manipulate
the facades to reduce the apparent scale.

On the inside, too, today's traditional architects are challenging the
idea that bigger or higher is better. Satisfying proportions are essential, even
when rooms are grand. The sequencing of rooms, the creation of internal
axial views, and the craft of materials become more important than square
footage for the sake of footage. Efforts are aimed as well at giving rooms the
integrity of historical houses, even while the closets, walk-in bars, baths,
dressing rooms, office alcoves, and other modern functional elements are
accommodated.

These issues of design—knowing the rules and how to apply them in
diverse situations—are not peculiarly Southern. But fold in climate, site

conditions, local architectural traditions, plus other factors, and a distinctive regional character begins to emerge. For example, the traditional openness of the Southern house, though no longer as important with full climate control, will be seen in light-filled galleries that reach out to embrace a terrace or garden. And though it may not be easy to pin down, the sociability of the South still largely dictates that the house be welcoming but not pretentious. As illustration, some years ago the owners of a house near the South Carolina coast had a new wing built while they were abroad. On return, they found it too much and had it taken down and rebuilt behind a bank of magnolias.

Different expressions of regional qualities in residential design derive from many sources. Present-day architects are looking closely at what their counterparts did in the District of Columbia, Asheville, Charleston, or Houston during the late nineteenth and early twentieth centuries. This exploration looks at both house and site, the latter very often dealing with the much larger impact of the automobile in today's residential design.

The South also has seen major acceptance of new neighborhood- or development-wide design standards and guidelines. It is a process introduced through the region's many local historic districts established over the past few decades. Now, controls on the placement, massing, and architectural character of new houses go far beyond those for a typical subdivision. For environmentally conscious developments along the coast or in the mountains, deference to setting might mean houses are disassociated from their street frontage or hidden from view and protected by forest cover.

ABOVE, RIGHT & OPPOSITE: *Above a sweep of lawn leading down to a beautiful Alabama lake, residential architects McAlpine-Tankersley designed a sophisticated take on the rustic lodge with giant stripped pine tree columns supporting the roof of the two-story central living area, exposed rafter-tails, stained shingle walls, and crisp white trim. The stair to an upper-level lookout speaks of the high degree of craft realized throughout.*

146

LEFT: *Drawing on the continued viability of the classical tradition, Mississippi-based architect Ken Tate translates this lasting language into an orderly sequence of bays overlooking a pool for a client in Jackson. At the client's request, the design evokes French classical Art Deco.*

BELOW: *In the hands of the late Frank McCall Jr., who revived a practice focused on fine period houses across South Georgia and beyond, the same care in design lavished on great mansions also extended to versions of Southern vernacular farmhouses, like this relaxed classical house in Moultrie, Georgia. Neil Turner of McCall-Turner continues the work.*

ABOVE: *Drawing on Mediterranean architecture often used in earlier houses there, Dallas architect Larry Boerder used color-washed stucco walls, arcades, and a terra-cotta tile roof with deep overhangs for light-and-shadow contrast.*

RIGHT: *For a fresh interpretation of the classical, Atlanta interior designers Gandy/Peace employ square columns, deep ceiling recesses, and light neutral colors to establish a serene and timeless flow of space. Sconces and other furnishings strike a classical/ contemporary balance.*

RIGHT: *Taking advantage of South Florida's continuing use of solid masonry construction, Miami architect Jorge Hernandez gets rich light-and-shadow effects from deep openings in an arcade and dramatic color washed on the walls of an inset portico.*

OPPOSITE: *In response to climate, Charleston Single Houses were shaped to catch prevailing breezes off the water.*

PREVIOUS PAGE: *The full revival of Southern style is in evidence in this row of recent houses designed by Georgia architect Jim Strickland to face the green at Newpoint near Beaufort, South Carolina. The development's code mandates porches and classical proportions as seen in a street of smaller houses nearby.*

An example of the growing number of neotraditional, new urbanist developments is Duany Plater-Zyberk's development in Seaside, Florida, where explicit rules require porches, proper proportion, appropriate materials, and other features to assure that houses are both distinctive and appropriate to the region. As they are built, these concentrations of tradition-based residential designs serve as compelling models for others to follow. Though it is a vacation town, Seaside has generated a new appreciation of well-designed, traditional houses for people building all across the South.

The historical period that produced the region's most singular domestic landmarks will not return, nor would we want it to, and much that is built today could truly be anyplace. But the current revival of fine residential design drawing on these and other sources of inspiration has put the South firmly back in touch with its deeper cultural heritage. It's about style, certainly, but it's also about something deeply felt and sustaining. A lofty porch open to a garden. A comfortably proportioned room with friends or family waiting for dinner. At home in the South.

CHAPTER VI

Gardens

To follow the tradition of bloom in three seasons only is to miss the full meaning of gardening in a part of the world where at all times of the year there are days when it is good to be out of doors, when there is work to be done in the garden, and when there is some plant in perfection of flower or fruit.

—Elizabeth Lawrence, *A Southern Garden*

ABOVE: *Creeping fig crowns a water spirit ornament. Tucked into the walls and corners in this Dallas garden, visual surprises keep the visitor guessing.*

OPPOSITE: *White and blue thunbergia cascade from the pergola behind this Coconut Grove, Florida, residence. Deck chairs, mottled stone, and olive jars suggest a court-yard in Provence.*

THE NATURAL WORLD NOURISHES THE SOUTHERN IDENTITY. We will always have a peculiarly intimate relationship with the land, with the spirit and the soil. And so a Southern garden is defined by far more than climate and species. The same herb and vegetable gardens that flourished more than one hundred years ago produce profusely today. The fresh flowers that are so accessible in our tame environment come indoors from container and planted gardens to fill our interior rooms and remind us of the landscape just a step—and sometimes a lifetime—away.

One whiff of the acrid scent of English ivy casts us back to childhood, when vine-shrouded walls of a country house in the mountains gave off a particular odor that came to be permanently associated with summer vaca-tions. The recollection is powerful. It triggers other sense memories—the way the dust dances in the sunbeams slanting through magnolia branches, the arrival of a riot of colors when azaleas emerge in early spring.

In the garden, a Southerner has one hand on the past while the other reaches for the future. We are reminded of seasons past, when the tree line was lower, when light fell differently. We remember the rose garden before the hurricane or the hydrangea bush ten years ago, when it was first

ABOVE: *Twelve hornbeam trees form a living house that frames Rob Jones's fiberglass* Ghost *sculpture.*

OPPOSITE, ABOVE: *Some of these hollyhocks grow ten feet tall. The gardener throws an annual party in an outdoor room he's created that comes to life when the hollyhocks reach peak perfection.*

OPPOSITE, BELOW: *A little circular area serves as a foyer to the hollyhock room.*

planted. The garden is a place where faith, hope, and optimism are renewed each spring, when we try something new, or correct a flaw. The completion of an interior design project does not inspire such emotional lows and highs, such triumphs of will and ingenuity over nature's capriciousness. A highboy cannot get blackspot. A table does not wilt. No tears will be shed over arranging a mantel. How could inanimate objects evoke the giddying triumph of the rose garden's first bloom in spring, each blossom textbook perfect. We look at the garden and see ourselves—the perilous pull toward chaos, the barely maintained order, the promise of excellence. It is never perfect. We are never finished.

In *Mrs. Whaley and Her Charleston Garden*, the late, great gardener Emily Whaley ruminated on life and gardens. She reflected, "A garden pushed back the wilderness. A garden was an intimate ground safe from lions and elephants and whatever else was out there. It was a safe place outside." One of the most basic human needs, the need for security, is fulfilled when we can look across an expanse of lawn, a flower border, or a little kitchen garden and revel in our tenuous victory over nature.

The balance between order and chaos is perilous at best. Southern landscape designers share a host of common enemies. Ben Page, of Nashville, Tennessee, creates some of the region's most spectacular gardens, and yet even he bemoans the obstacles. "Weather, bugs, soil, drainage," he says, reciting a discouraging list of conditions. Most gardeners aspire to organic gardening, offering tips on buried beer mugs (to catch slugs) and mail-order ladybugs. And yet, almost all confess to an annual lapse of principle, when the pests become so fierce that the desperate gardener longs to douse the whole yard in toxic chemicals. Allen Lacy, a Texan by birth and now a columnist for the *New York Times*, acknowledges his own weakness in his book, *The Inviting Garden*: "Were Monsanto or Dow to come up with

something that would rid our garden of slugs, instantly and forever, I would be sorely tempted indeed."

Wet, often freezing winters give way to long blazing summers in the South, providing challenges at both ends of the growing season. Mild spring days change abruptly to bitter cold or even snow. Weeks of drought might be followed by weeks of rain, proving that in the South, the weather is even more corrupt than the politicians. There inevitably comes a moment when the gardener longs for a penthouse apartment, free from the responsibility of anything larger than a terra-cotta pot. Either we sink slowly into despair, or we recognize that this conflict, like so many others, brings its own satisfactions.

Because one fine day, the weather breaks, the sun emerges, a cool breeze sweeps away the haze, or the garden revives under a steady afternoon

shower. Many little things can renew hope in the undaunted gardener. To be sure, the first crocus of spring makes nearly everyone's heart beat a bit faster.

To generalize about the Southern garden is to miss the richness and variety of the different regions, which can vary widely from north to south and east to west. According to the American Horticultural Society, the South spans five of its growing zones—zones six through ten—which gives the Southern garden five distinct personalities.

Every city in the region has a particular plant that the visitor will forever associate with that place and always regret trying to establish at home. Oleander looks temptingly lush against a Charleston garden wall, but it will not survive a Tennessee winter. Rhododendron means Cashiers, North Carolina, in June. Wisteria is Birmingham in April. Bougainvillea? Palm Beach, year-round.

Each place has a particular style of gardening as well. The small courtyard garden is as indigenous to Charleston as the oleander. Nashville is rolling woodlands. In Palm Beach, ficus hedges tower overhead, concealing a swimming pool, while bougainvillea dangles from hanging pots near the seating area around the pool. In New Orleans, there is a marvelous hybrid of French and tropical plantings—banana plants, palms, and jasmine juxtaposed with potted lemon trees and rosemary.

In horse country, places like Middleburg, Virginia, and Lexington, Kentucky, landscapes of rolling hills invite galloping and jumping. Green meadows lie just beyond garden gates, a constant reminder of the sporting life. In the mountains of North Carolina, little English gardens nestle in the curve of the mountainside, oblivious to the vertiginous vista all around. In the historic woodlands of Maryland, vast grounds are ordered into outdoor rooms linked by archways laden with roses.

In Dallas, where neighboring Mexico lends an air of exoticism, the swimming pool is often carved into the landscape like the Italian villa's courtyard. Charleston's rich history, with the French arriving on the heels of English settlers, spawned a mingled garden style. Tiny courtyards enclose strictly ordered outdoor rooms with an English taste for flourishing hard

ABOVE: *French elements abound in the landscape of a Virginia farmhouse. A clipped boxwood garden forms a visual boundary between it and the rolling landscape beyond.*

OPPOSITE, ABOVE: *Trim boxwoods lend Italian flair to a Dallas garden. The precise, symmetrical arrangement of four pots gives a French sense of order to the fountain.*

plantings fronted by colorful borders. Espaliered shrubs coexist with perennials in a distinctive mix.

The many plants associated with a specific region allow gardeners to commune directly with their roots, their own customs. The azalea border in the Middle South—Alabama, Tennessee, Mississippi, and Georgia—produces its spectacular display early in the spring, providing the first abundant table arrangements of the gardening year.

And while mention of the South conjures up lush images of flowers blooming in abundance, our trees that blossom over the course of the year have also come to be closely identified with the region. The magnolia tree's waxy leaves give birth to lush blossoms whose soft white color is as fleeting as a cool summer day. The dogwoods and the cherry trees burst into sweet songs in early spring, their white and pale pink blossoms summoning tourists

to the nation's capital in search of organic, rather than political, antics. And the camellia tree colors our winters with flowers that some consider more lush than the roses of summer.

As far as fall color is concerned, our autumns may not spawn the riot of shades that come to life in New England, but North Carolina and Virginia turn a luscious rainbow of reds, oranges, and yellows, while the evergreens keep their cool color, giving the palette of the South a richness and diversity second to none. And across the South Carolina Low Country and bayous of Louisiana, oak trees draped with Spanish moss, evoking the history and humidity of the region, have become symbols of the Southern United States.

FRENCH LESSONS

Although English garden design has a powerful grip on the imagination, the French influence is growing rapidly and has a firm hold in Creole Louisiana, where roses, poppies, lilies, phlox, and coreopsis fill geometrically shaped and highly ordered flower beds. Symmetry, exactitude, and control distinguish the French garden. With its subtle, abstract qualities, it serves as an intellectual experience as much as a sensual one.

André Le Nôtre's designs for the gardens at Versailles embodied the sovereign philosophy of Louis XIV and remain the penultimate example of the French formal landscape. Southern gardeners reproducing the French ideal replicate the inspired style of the celebrated French landscape architect, but on a much more intimate scale. The sculptures and pools that pay tribute

BELOW, LEFT: *Privet hedges divided by gravel paths form an old-fashioned parterre. Antique roses, balsam, and, in the center, a pineapple keep company.*

BELOW, RIGHT: *Weathered cypress fences were gathered from the surrounding Louisiana countryside to form the perimeter of this garden. A coral vine clings to the pickets.*

to and reflect the beauty of the architecture at the French chateau find renewed expression throughout the South in modest antique garden figures, whose charm respects the majesty of the statues surrounding Versailles. Here, petite pools of water gaze back at flowers and plants, making small gardens seem larger and large ones even more grand. And a *tapis vert* (literally, green rug) blankets flat expanses of earth, inviting visitors and residents to sit and picnic or nap, and in some areas, play a game of croquet.

The far-reaching sightlines at Versailles afforded the king a view of his domain extending literally as far as the eye could see. In a tribute to him, nature bowed in servitude to man. The parterre gardens in particular, with their low, manicured hedges, were intentionally flat so that the king might view them from the windows of the palace. Translated into the landscape, the parterre beds are separated by pea gravel paths that crunch distinctively underfoot. They are one aspect of French gardens that Southerners have sincerely embraced. The feeling of belonging in the garden magnifies with the tactile experience of walking on shifting, responsive gravel. As a practical matter, gravel eliminates the need for coddling and maintenance of all-over grass, which has its own appeal in a region where maintaining grass can be problematic due to uneven sunlight and brutal temperatures.

ENGLISH ROOTS

The profuse, colorful border is the most captivating English garden influence, as gardeners adapt it to the Southern climate and soil. The rose hedge, soft in its edges; the sense of permanence from well-established plants; the neat grassy pathways through the growth—all are hallmarks of the Anglophile's garden. Vita Sackville-West's Sissinghurst is the Versailles of English gardens. When she described its plan, "strictest formality of design with the maximum informality in planting," she might as well have described the ideal Southern garden.

One of the most alluring qualities of English garden design is that plantings are mixed—roses set among the perennials—so long as the color combination works. The natural plant shape reigns supreme, with pruning limited to only what is necessary for the health of the plant. Branches flop; rose petals litter the lawn; abundance is rewarded.

An English garden invites a walk. Where a French garden might impress and surprise with its never-ending vistas, an English garden strives to excite, to inspire to improve. Seating, the most important concession to human comfort, encourages rest and peaceful contemplation of the garden.

ABOVE: *In a North Carolina garden, blueberries for cutting and eating grow among the flowers and shrubs.*

OPPOSITE: *A charming playhouse in a Maryland garden gets fairytale treatment with an old-fashioned climbing rose. Pink peonies echo the color of the New Dawn roses that bloom above them.*

The benches, swings, hammocks, and chairs that Southerners place in their gardens bear witness to the pleasure of solitary appreciation of the work.

The mix of textures, contrasting leaf shapes, and shades of green provides gardeners with subtle modes of expression. The ferns that grow so well in the South invite juxtaposition with the broader-leafed hosta. Where shade is necessary for respite from the sun, or unavoidable due to a high dense canopy, the undaunted gardener takes heart from noted English garden authority Rosemary Verey's early writings on her garden: "As for plants I must get to know them, so I can choose them to suit their sites as well as their neighbors."

What seems to be achieved so effortlessly in England is hard won in the South. The soil always seems to have too much or too little of whatever a particular plant needs to survive. "You can generally accommodate weather, but with soil, you're fighting against Mother Nature," says Ben Page. And then, even when the garden is nestled under a couture blend of

ABOVE: *White pompom dahlias in a Blowing Rock, North Carolina, garden lift their globe-shaped heads in the perennial bed.*

RIGHT, ABOVE: *A shaft of sunlight finds its way through the dense mountaintop canopy.*

RIGHT, BELOW: *Like a fairytale cottage, this English-style garden offers respite from the summer heat. Two pillars of local stone flank the entryway. Grassy paths meander through perennial beds.*

OPPOSITE: *Plantings of hosta, echinacea, and lamb's ear showcase a variety of Southerners' favorite plants.*

peat, soil, and manure, along comes an April hard freeze, thick layers of ice coating every tender green shoot, delivering death in ghastly silence.

Worms and insects can be just as menacing. For example, the New Dawn rose on an arbor may bud in great profusion. The leaves might be dark and glossy, bursting with good health. The proud gardener will admire the payoff of her labor in the misty morning, only to notice the unmistakable affront of a caterpillar's ravenous handiwork on the remaining half a bud. Of course, caterpillars are the price we pay for butterflies later on.

Gardening is not a weekend pastime. There is too much work to be done simply fighting the weather, insects, and disease. Landscape designers insist that their clients be willing to spend at least a little time in the garden to expect good results. "There is no such thing as low-maintenance gardening," says Ryan Gainey, Atlanta's award-winning landscape designer and

ABOVE: *In this romantic garden in Delaware's Brandywine River valley, a twenty-four-foot-wide border of hollyhocks forms the walls that embrace a section of pasture.*

OPPOSITE: *Carved out of the woodlands of Columbus, Georgia, this English-style garden, composed on a series of terraces over the hillside, stands in stark contrast to the surrounding wilderness. The garden's concentric circles urge the eye to the center, where a giant French fountain basin topped with yucca and thyme reigns over all.*

author. "There is such a thing as less maintenance. You need to ask yourself if gardening is really a part of your lifestyle."

There is a difference between the people who love to really get their hands dirty and those who prefer stand at a safe distance and point with a long stick. Both take credit for their gardens' well-being. The former may be recognized by the smugly superior look on his face, and the dirt under his fingernails. Elizabeth Lawrence, the legendary Southern garden writer, makes a good case for the proxy gardener: "The gardener must be willing to study as well as to dig."

PORCHES, TERRACES, AND GAZEBOS

As much as our gardens are extensions of our houses, the terraces and porches are of supreme importance. They provide transition between the indoors and the outdoors, bridging the distance, both figurative and literal, between the sheltered interior and the partial wilderness beyond the doors. The terrace is where the garden meets the house. The furniture from inside is echoed in the tables, chairs, and benches we put on terraces. The garden sends representatives in the colorful pots we place around the seating. Begonias, in their shade-loving glory, can be moved out of the sun. Boxwoods can be fed and nurtured in their pots, and moved out of the way for parties. Stones that emerge during construction or simple digging across the region, but most particularly in Texas, Arkansas, and Oklahoma, find new

A series of descending garden terraces structures the vast grounds in this Birmingham garden. The homeowner sought help from the local botanical gardens to restore the garden with historical integrity.

life as steps from the terrace to the garden or as pathways when gravel is not appropriate.

With warm weather extending over so much of the year, Southerners can enjoy their evening meal outside quite often. The terrace, with its concessions to comfort—a flat surface to steady table and chair legs—and proximity to the kitchen, makes entertaining outdoors a natural impulse. In Texas, the outdoor dining room often includes a fireplace for outdoor entertaining year-round.

Southerners may not have invented the porch, but they have certainly perfected it. In a climate that keeps people indoors for much of the summer, the porch offers sanctuary from the heat and proximity to comforts indoors. The family gathers on the porch on Sunday afternoons to watch the neighborhood pass by on the sidewalk out front. Confrontations, confessions, and reconciliations take place in this semiprivate space.

WATER

One of the most common features in gardens, whether they be in South Florida or in northern Virginia, is a fountain. The sight of moving water, and most important, the sound of its rippling cascade, take the heat out of a hot summer day almost magically. In a place where gardening is enjoyed year-round, the splash and burble of a fountain can brighten a winter day and keep alive the promise of spring.

A stream meandering through a garden responds to a rainfall by swelling and rushing in frantic reaction to the heavens' gift. Drifting petals and falling leaves find their way onto the water's surface, spinning in the breeze, performing an intricate dance to nature's rhythm. The course of

BELOW: *Hosta and dianthus provide contrasting leaf texture. An abundant oakleaf hydrangea towers over the pathway.*

NEXT PAGE: *A white garden in Birmingham features daisies, stock, and lamb's ear around a fountain. At night the white flowers glow in the moonlight.*

RIGHT: *An iron gate opens into a tropical paradise. A border of Mexican sage, red Java glory bower, and areca palms frames the lily pond in a Palm Beach garden.*

OPPOSITE: *In Mexico, innumerable pots of geraniums and impatiens surround a pool, where jacaranda blossoms from the nearby trees float on the water. The splash of water falling from stone horses cools the hot summer air.*

the stream may change, curving more tightly into the landscape, or pooling in a glade. Time makes its mark, etching the passing of the years over the mutable earth.

The best moments in the garden occur in private. Much pinching back of plants occurs over morning coffee. The smell of the garden warming under the rising summer sun imbues us with a deep sense of well-being. From proprietorship of these lands comes a sense of responsibility and investiture. As much as we look at our children and dimly see the promise of our legacy, we can look to our gardens and trace our lives in the turning of the seasons.

CHAPTER VII

Preservation

The roof came down steep and black like a cowl, reaching out beyond the wide galleries that encircled the yellow stuccoed house. Big, solemn oaks grew close to it, and their thick-leaved, far-reaching branches shadowed it like a pall.

—Kate Chopin, "Désirée's Baby"

ABOVE: *Built as a town house by John Tayloe III and his wife, Ann, this structure became a winter residence for the couple in 1801. With a bowed entrance anchoring its important corner location, the building, later named the Octagon, can be seen on New York Avenue in Washington, D.C.*

OPPOSITE: *The Octagon's empty dining room features all the architectural detailing that makes the house an important example of Federal architecure and a source for historic and architectural study.*

AMERICA'S HISTORIC PRESERVATION MOVEMENT WAS BORN in the South, and most of the advances that have shaped it took root in Southern soil. After a slow start, partly because of the prevalent perception of America as a new land without a deep history, the movement has taken hold and is gaining in strength. Preservation's early focus, at the end of the last century, stressed patriotism and the creation of shrines to the nation's founders. It has since evolved to include the homes of less well known figures whose personal properties are a source of learning and inspiration to current scholars and students of history. And to an even greater extent, the preservation movement has reached those private citizens who view ownership of historic properties as a sort of stewardship and who take responsibility for the property's role in the development of past and future cultural traditions.

THE MOVEMENT'S BEGINNINGS

Fittingly, the first successful national effort began when a developer threatened to turn George Washington's Mount Vernon into a hotel. Neither the federal government nor the state of Virginia would buy the estate. So in 1854 Ann Pamela Cunningham stepped in. A small, frail spinster from an upcountry South Carolina plantation, she appealed to the women of the

South and took the first step toward Mount Vernon's purchase. Cunningham's Mount Vernon Ladies' Association of the Union, one of the country's first successful preservation organizations, became a blueprint that many preservation organizations around the country subsequently tried to emulate. It was a tightly organized body that embraced publicity as a tool and canvased the entire country for support and contributions.

As the nineteenth century wound down and American critics began associating early American architecture with high moral purpose, aesthetics became accepted as a criterion for preservation. Ever a tool of reformers, the preservation movement expressed a growing discomfort with the conspicuous consumption of the Gilded Age. The movement believed that exposing the public to simple, rugged old houses would inspire more substantive values. And when the turn of the century brought waves of new immigrants onto American shores, educator-preservationists promoted their cause in an effort to assimilate newcomers. Meanwhile, a recently established middle class soothed its anxieties about the newcomers by embracing a veneration of the American past.

Building on the example of Mount Vernon, early preservation efforts made museums out of buildings that were associated with famous men. There was the Lee Mansion in Arlington, Virginia, and, of course,

One of the finest examples of Creole architecture, the circa 1790 Whitney Plantation in Saint John the Baptist Parish, Louisiana, was once a profitable sugar plantation. It features a loggia and galleries, which were used as outdoor rooms, particularly in the heat of summer.

A trompe l'oeil niche at Whitney Plantation depicts a small cherub, or putto, sitting atop an urn. Though faded over time, the mural is clearly inspired by the frescoes of classical antiquity and the eighteenth-century excavations at Pompeii and Herculaneum.

Monticello. Purchased in 1836, Jefferson's home in Charlottesville languished during more than eighty years of litigation before finally being saved in the late 1920s. Monticello was the first restoration to be valued not only for its historic and patriotic significance but also for its architectural significance as a preeminent example of classical design, one of the strongest influences on the evolution of American styles.

During the early decades of the new century, two efforts undertaken in the South brought profound nationwide changes in preservation and laid the groundwork for the future. One was a museum-oriented reconstruction of an entire eighteenth-century town, Virginia's Colonial Williamsburg, which endowed preservation with a new professionalism and brought men into what had been a mostly female and volunteer activity. At about the same time, the work on historic Charleston, South Carolina, extended preservation's purview beyond museum-oriented restorations and reconstructions to embrace entire living neighborhoods. Charleston established the nation's first historic district in 1931 and provided America's first preservation ordinance;

this ordinance, implemented by a board of architectural review, regulated the appearance of properties and injected government into what had been a movement of private individuals. Charleston preservationists also introduced the revolving fund, which allows preservation organizations to purchase and restore historic buildings, sell them, and then use the proceeds to rescue still more old buildings.

North Carolina and Georgia have made productive use of the revolving fund concept as they rescue old buildings in an effort to reclaim the best assets of the South's problematic past. In fact, many Southern cities, in struggling to recover from the devastation of the Civil War and the Depression, reinvented their economies in large part, taking advantage of the potential for tourism.

Efforts to preserve historic Charleston and other historic Southern cities were aided by a side effect of America's increasing interest in art and architecture. Museum-sponsored expeditions in search of period rooms headed south. Because industrialization had bypassed the region—and also, perhaps, because Southerners were more passionately attached to their past—most preindustrial enclaves in the South remained intact.

Especially during the boom and bust years of the 1920s and 1930s, the South's relatively stagnant economy nurtured several national preservation efforts, nearly all of which benefited from the inclusion of preservation in federal government policy. The Historic American Buildings Survey (HABS)

ABOVE: *The denticulated cornice, wraparound mantel, and decorated overmantel at Whitney Plantation were probably added around 1803, as was the house's other woodwork decoration. It was embellished with faux bois, faux marble, and gilding.*

RIGHT: *Whitney Plantation was built by Jean Jacques Haydel Sr. around 1790, and the faux painting was commissioned by Marcellin Haydel between 1836 and 1839. The elaborate ceiling cartouche features the initials M. and H. as a tribute to the house's owner at the time.*

started in the winter of 1934–35; the Depression-era New Deal recovery programs provided funding; and the Historic Sites Act of 1935 designated the National Park Service as the government's preservation agency. But the most abiding influence on preservation in the South was Charleston's example. Charleston's preservation ordinance, for instance, was the model for that of New Orleans, which protected the Vieux Carré—the French Quarter. By 1937 the rescue of the French Quarter was ensured after an epic fight by preservationists through an amendment to the state constitution. It empowered the city to create a commission with broad policing powers and the authority to exempt historic properties from taxation. Another first.

In San Antonio, a group of dedicated artists led an effort similar to that carried out in Charleston. Although the San Antonio Conservation Society was founded in 1924 by Rena Maverick Green, a descendant of Texas patriot Sam Maverick, it was the author and art teacher Emily Edwards who became the group's leader and spearheaded a movement that transformed the San Antonio River from a menace in times of flood into the city's major asset, the famed Riverwalk. The city also led the effort to retrieve America's Spanish past and introduce festivals and other forms of entertainment to gain support and raise funds.

Natchez, Mississippi's contribution to the preservation movement—pilgrimages to a grand past—was no exception to the rule that each Southern city's preservation effort was local and largely singular. Natchez's

RIGHT: *This 1874 Italianate Savannah residence was covered in dark brown paint, but a careful study of guidelines offered options that allowed the homeowners to select a beige stucco facade with lighter beige wood trim and garnet front doors in restoring it. Cities throughout the South are finding that color, as well as structural, guidelines can be helpful in preserving the spirit of an area.*

OPPOSITE: *In an attempt to preserve the historic character of the area, a former vacant lot in Savannah, Georgia, was filled in with a pair of single-family houses. The facade view illustrates the two essential factors in successful traditional design: proper proportions and attention to detail.*

proudest possession was a series of Federal and Greek Revival houses spectacularly sited to evoke romantic notions of the antebellum past. In 1929 the persuasive Katherine Miller convinced her husband to buy one of the earliest houses and held the first of her annual pilgrimages. Held every spring and fall, the pilgrimages are essentially house tours that have become fixtures on the Southern calendar.

In Florida, St. Augustine's preservation history took a different turn. During the Depression, the Carnegie Institution in Washington, D.C., sent a distinguished retired National Park Service historian, Verne Chatelaine, to head a restoration program with help from the New Deal's Works Progress Administration. Predictably, disagreements between local groups and professional outsiders held up passage of a zoning ordinance until the 1950s. Still affected by the delay, St. Augustine's historic structures are interrupted by touristy retail establishments that don't always respect the architectural style of the city. An active preservation organization is trying to turn things around, but St. Augustine may never regain the time it lost.

During the early postwar years, preservation in the South, as elsewhere, was shaped by opposition to two federal government initiatives. The Housing and Home Finance Agency, later the Department of Housing and Urban Development, started an urban renewal program, which swept away old buildings to make way for the new. And the Department of Transportation's ancestor, the Bureau of Public Roads, rammed expressways through many historic neighborhoods and abetted a massive flight to the suburbs with its interstate roadway program.

No city in the nation fought the battle for postwar preservation more valiantly than Savannah, Georgia. Concern for the city's architecture and founder James Edward Oglethorpe's eighteenth-century plan of green city squares became critical when the downtown was all but abandoned. In 1954 seven local women founded the Historic Savannah Foundation in response to two immediate threats. Developers wanted to convert the City Market into a parking garage and to pave the squares on Habersham Street to make a through boulevard.

Led by Lee Adler, the son of one of the foundation's founders (and a recurring figure in John Berendt's *Midnight in the Garden of Good and Evil*), Savannah preservationists succeeded in reclaiming more than one thousand dilapidated downtown mansions and row houses, one by one, through the use of a revolving fund. They have lured upper-middle-class citizens back into the city, reclaimed the waterfront, replanted open spaces, and shifted their attention to adjacent historic neighborhoods. The foundation sold the idea of preservation as vigorously as Coca-Cola sells soft drinks, inventorying the two-and-one-half-mile downtown to gain support by illustrating the vastness of the project; publishing promotional materials; working with the Chamber of Commerce to promote tourism; and persuading city officials to use urban renewal funds for conservation and preservation. Savannah's successes drew activists from as near as Columbus, Georgia; Shreveport, Louisiana; and Roanoke, Virginia; and as far as San Antonio and Galveston—a city blessed with a historic cast-iron district known as the Strand. They mainly learned to avoid conventional development formulas, to stress the retention of local character, and to involve neighborhood residents.

The federal government has played a contradictory role. While spawning programs that threatened historic resources, it has also provided the means to brake the speed and scale with which historic resources are obliterated. Congress chartered the National Trust for Historic Preservation in 1949 and, as part of Lyndon Johnson's Great Society legislation, passed the National Historic Preservation Act in 1966. That legislation provided funding, placed a new scientific emphasis on restoration methods and classifications, increased public awareness of preservation issues, and was intended to "give a sense of orientation to our society, using structures and objects of the past to establish values of time and place," said William J. Murtagh, the first keeper of the National Register of Historic Places (*Keeping Time:*

OPPOSITE & ABOVE: *The central hall of the Moore-Gwyn house in North Carolina features a handsome carved staircase. Once used as a barn, the house has benefited from the state's attempt to place old houses in private hands. It was restored in the 1940s, and many fine features, including the staircase and several ornately carved mantels, were saved.*

The History and Theory of Preservation in America, Main Street Press, 1988). Significantly, Johnson's secretary of the interior, Stewart L. Udall, soon decentralized government responsibility for preservation by establishing preservation offices in each of the fifty states. The National Trust, meanwhile, nurtured the growth of first local and then statewide affiliates. And grassroots preservation groups proliferated throughout the South.

Preservation was given an additional boost during the 1970s with the rise of the environmental movement, of which it is an integral part; by the energy crisis, which encouraged a back-to-the-city movement; by the patriotic bicentennial celebrations of 1976, which focused interest on history and heritage; and by tax incentives the same year that promoted preservation (they were largely rescinded in the 1980s).

Once primarily a tool for saving high-style European-derived architecture, the preservation movement has widened its embrace to ordinary industrial and commercial buildings, to the commercial districts of smaller towns, to urban residential neighborhoods, and to Main Streets. More controversially, preservation has also stretched its concerns to such issues as promoting cultural diversity. The National Trust has focused attention on sprawl, which National Trust for Historic Preservation director Richard Moe says is "to current preservationists what urban renewal was to an earlier generation."

He believes that Americans are increasingly aware that outlying areas cannot thrive if their inner cities languish.

In recent years, historic preservation has become an engine for economic development, notably through tourism in a growing number of historic districts. This also raises the specter of tourists overwhelming fragile historic neighborhoods. A more insidious threat is a growing property rights movement, which interprets the imposition of almost any land-use regulation on private property as a "taking" without compensation in violation of the Fifth Amendment.

Preservationists are facing these and other questions in a spirit pioneered and tested by the movement as it developed in the South. Grassroots groups, led by individuals intent on learning from history and example, are examining and applying available lessons in ways that speak to their own environs.

THE IMPACT

These groups have been successful thoughout the South, transforming neglected and underresearched properties into sources of learning and inspiration. From entire neighborhoods to specific domestic and civic architecture to private interiors, the efforts of grassroots preservation groups around the

Sometime in the late nineteenth century, Moravian painter Naaman Reich added three trompe l'oeil window niches to the parlor of his Bethania, North Carolina, home. A still life of flowers and fruit sits between faux stone walls over the fireplace.

Careful cleaning uncovered the details of a 150-year-old painted ceiling medallion in the Reich-Butner house near Winston-Salem, North Carolina. Shaded paint strokes imitate the sculptural curve of fashionable molded plaster.

country have rescued our youthful past from total obscurity. And in rescuing our past, we have learned things about it—the kinds of plates and glasses used, uncovered during archaeological excavations; the layout of slave quarters, which we knew little about before such digs took place; the evolution of a house that may start out as Federal and become Palladian as tastes and fashions change; and even trends revealed through investigations of wall coverings.

Neighborhoods in particular can be compelling settings in which to revisit the past. Savannah succeeded with the help of a set of guidelines that instruct any restoration work done residentially and commercially in the city. Louisville, Kentucky, maintains the same sort of control over its St. James and Belgravia Streets in the historic district, preserving the past for the future. And Beaufort, South Carolina, has caught up with Charleston in its preservation of pre-Revolutionary and pre–Civil War sites. By vigilantly

preventing any encroachment and actively encouraging a spirit that respects the contemporary relevance of old properties, whole areas can be maintained and utilized. While Virginia's Colonial Williamsburg provides a glimpse into life in Colonial America, the lure of living in a preserved historic building, albeit with contemporary conveniences, is much more seductive.

The discoveries that come with careful preservation of private and public properties instruct the present. One example is the 1819 Owens-Thomas House in Savannah, which was suffering from loose stucco, neglected ironwork, and eighty thousand tourists a year. Generally considered one of the finest examples of English Regency architecture in this country, the house was designed by English architect William Jay in 1816. Constructed with native material, such as tabby—a combination of lime, sand, and oyster shells—the house also had one remarkable feature that was overlooked until a recent restoration. Workers uncovered long-hidden details of a nearly intact domestic plumbing system that was original to the construction date. It included indoor cisterns, water closets, lead and ceramic pipes, sinks and baths, even a shower. Such conveniences were miraculously advanced for their time. In addition, a study of the layers of paint on the interior walls disclosed elaborate, previously unknown finishes. Decorative trompe l'oeil, wood grain finishes, and colors, such as bright lime green, came to light.

A little more than a decade earlier, in the 1970s, the curators at Colonial Williamsburg had begun to suspect that the misty, autumnal colors that we associate with the last two centuries were actually much more intense than originally believed. In essence, whispery blues were actually a rich Prussian blue; faded brick was closer to raspberry jam; and the earthy maize recognized as eighteenth-century yellow began as an egg yolk gold. Scholars now identify those grayed colors not with the eighteenth century, but with the Colonial Revival style that became popular with the restoration of Colonial Williamsburg in the 1920s. Thorough investigations of wallpaper and layers of paint have now revealed the original colors, which are confirmed with a look at the ceramics and fabrics that survive to this day. Pastel was not the tone of choice in the eighteenth century, and curators have taken note.

Similarly, in private houses around the country, homeowners are taking the time to learn more about their own properties and are discovering the kinds of things that showed up at the Owens-Thomas House and Colonial Williamsburg. Investigations in Louisiana and North Carolina have revealed a whole history of interior decorative painting that included faux bois—or false wood graining—and marbleizing. Even in modest properties, there seems to have been an awareness of and appreciation for the more fancy

ABOVE: *A sharp clear green that evokes the color of grass in springtime now covers the dining room walls at Colonial Williamsburg's Wythe House. The taste for green in the eighteenth century is proven by the plates and fabrics that survive to this day.*

OPPOSITE: *As a result of thorough investigations of layers of paint and wallpaper, curators have learned that the colors of the past are not the faded colors we see today. Rather faded brick colors originally resembled this raspberry jam wall covering at Wythe House, and whispery blues were actually a rich Prussian blue.*

193

ornamentation that was occurring on a much grander scale in cities and in the region's iconic country estates. As more information is uncovered, we learn that we had more in common with our ancestors than we thought— a desire to improve and beautify our surroundings and an unwavering affinity for embracing eclectic style.

Armed with information about life in the Old South, we can do battle with the ravages of time and neglect. The Octagon, a premier example of American-Federal architecture built in Washington, D.C., in 1801, is a case study of the evolution of preservation in this country. The Octagon's first restoration took place in 1910, when the wood floor of the entrance hall was replaced with original black and white marble in a large diamond pattern. The second major work, between the 1920s and 1930s, focused on restoration of the basement plaster and trim. In the 1940s, a third effort substituted more durable Ohio sandstone for the surface of the deteriorating sandstone base. In response to structural problems, a fourth campaign, in 1954 and 1955, replaced most of the original second floor with a modern metal pan-and-steel framing system. And, to prepare the building for use as a house museum, a buildingwide renovation took place from 1968 to 1970.

But mechanical systems compromised the building fabric, and layers of paint still obscured details. Subsequent investigations revealed that the weight and rigidity of the steel structure inserted in the 1950s was causing masonry walls to crack. A $5 million nationwide campaign remedied the problem by funding a complete state-of-the-art restoration project.

As a result, the hipped roof, which early on replaced the original flat roof because it leaked, was restored with cypress shingles. The offending steel framing was removed and replaced with wood replicating the original. A new mechanical vault was placed underground between the house and sidewalk, freeing up the basement for restoration. Plaster and millwork were repaired, and finishes that could be determined were returned to those of the period.

The restoration of a historic property is an ongoing process, one that does not end with a year's worth of work. Like any organic being, a building breathes, expanding and contracting with the climate and the shifting of the earth's surface. As new discoveries are made, new problems in original architecture or later restoration work are uncovered. And the responsibility incumbent upon its inhabitants can be fiscally and emotionally daunting. But the rewards are limitless because historic properties speak of a time and a place. They contain voices from the past and faces for the future. In the South, they tell of old struggles and new promise in a region whose history is always present.

OPPOSITE: *At the Octagon, a rotunda-like entry opens to a central stair hall between splayed rectangular wings, with the dining room to the right, drawing room to the left. Details of the arched opening reflect the light, graceful character of American-Federal style and the comprehensive restoration that has preserved it.*

Southern
Historic Homes

ALABAMA

Gaineswood
805 S. Cedar Ave.
Demopolis, AL 36732
334/289-4846

Oakleigh House Museum
850 Oakleigh Place
Mobile, AL 36604
334/432-1281

Sturtivant Hall
713 Mabry St.
Selma, AL 36701
334/872-5626

DELAWARE

Nemours Mansion
and Gardens
1600 Rockland Rd.
Wilmington, DE 19803
302/651-6912

Winterthur Museum,
Garden, and Library
Winterthur, DE
302/888-4600

DISTRICT OF COLUMBIA

Decatur House
748 Jackson Place, NW
Washington, DC 20006
202/842-0920

Dumbarton House
2715 Q St., NW
Washington, DC 20007
202/337-2288

The Octagon
1799 New York Ave., NW
Washington, DC 20006-5292
202/638-3221

Tudor Place
1644 31st St., NW
Washington, DC 20007
202/965-0400

Woodrow Wilson House
2340 S Street, NW
Washington, DC 20008
202/387-4062

FLORIDA

Audubon House and Gardens
205 Whitehead St.
Key West, FL 33040
305/294-2116

Stranahan House
335 Southeast 6th Ave.
Fort Lauderdale, FL 33316
954/524-4736

Vizcaya Museum and Gardens
3251 S. Miami Ave.
Miami, FL 33129
305/250-9133

GEORGIA

Bulloch Hall
180 Bulloch Ave.
Roswell, GA 30075
770/992-1731

Herndon Home
587 University Pl., NW
Atlanta, GA 30314
404/581-9813

Owens-Thomas House
124 Abercorn St.
Savannah, GA 31401
912/233-9743

KENTUCKY

Ashland
120 Sycamore Rd.
Lexington, KY 40502
606/266-8581

Hunt-Morgan House
201 North Mill
Lexington, KY 40507
606/233-3290

Locust Grove
561 Blankenbaker Lane
Louisville, KY 40207
502/897-9845

Mary Todd Lincoln House
578 W. Main
Lexington, KY 40507
606/233-9999

Whitehall
3110 Lexington Rd.
Louisville, KY 40206
502/897-2944

LOUISIANA

Gallier House
1118–1132 Royal St.
New Orleans, LA 70116
504/525-5661

Hermann Grima House
820 St. Louis St.
New Orleans, LA 70112
504/525-5661

Longue Vue House
and Gardens
7 Bamboo Rd.
New Orleans, LA 70124
504/488-5488

Magnolia Mound Plantation
2161 Nicholson Dr.
Baton Rouge, LA 70802
225/343-4955

Oak Alley Plantation
3645 LA Highway 18
Vacherie, LA 70090
800/442-5539

Rosedown Plantation
and Historic Gardens
12501 Highway 10
St. Francisville, LA 70775
225/635-3332

Shadows-on-the-Teche
317 E. Main St.
New Iberia, LA 70560
318/369-6446

MARYLAND

Evergreen House
4545 N. Charles St.
Baltimore, MD 21210-2693
410/516-0341

Hammond-Harwood House
19 Maryland Ave.
Annapolis, MD 21401-1626
410/269-1714

Riversdale Mansion
4811 Riverdale Rd.
Riverdale Park, MD 20737
301/864-0420

MISSISSIPPI

Dunleith
84 Homochitto St.
Natchez, MS 39120
601/446-8500

Longwood House
140 Lower Woodville Rd.
Natchez, MS 39120
601/442-5193

Magnolia Hall
215 S. Pearl St.
Natchez, MS 39120
601/442-6672

Monmouth Plantation
36 Melrose Ave.
Natchez, MS 39120
601/442-5852

The Oaks House Museum
823 N. Jefferson St.
Jackson, MS 39202
601/353-9339

Stanton Hall
High at Pearl St.
Natchez, MS 39120
601/442-6282

NORTH CAROLINA

Ayr Mount
376 Saint Mary's Rd.
Hillsborough, NC 27278
919/732-6886

The Bellamy Mansion
503 Market St.
Wilmington, NC 28401
910/251-3700

Biltmore Estate
One N. Pack Square
Asheville, NC 28801
800/624-1575

Historic Rosedale
3427 N. Tryon St.
Charlotte, NC 28001
704/335-0325

Mordecai House
1 Mimosa St.
Raleigh, NC 27604
919/834-4844

Poplar Grove
Historic Plantation
Highway 17 North
Wilmington, NC 28405
910/686-9518

Reynolda House
2250 Reynolda Rd.
Winston-Salem, NC 27106
336/725-5325

SOUTH CAROLINA

Aiken-Rhett House
48 Elizabeth St.
Charleston, SC 29401
843/724-8481

Drayton Hall
3380 Ashley River Rd.
Charleston, SC 29414
843/766-0188

Magnolia Plantation
Route 4, Highway 61
Charleston, SC 29401
843/571-1266

Middleton Place
Ashley River Rd.
Charleston, SC 29414
843/556-6020

Nathaniel Russell House
51 Meeting St.
Charleston, SC 29401
843/724-8481

TENNESSEE

Belle Meade Plantation
5025 Harding Rd.
Nashville, TN 37205
615/356-0501

The Hermitage
4580 Rachels Lane
Hermitage, TN 37076
615/889-2941

Historic Carnton Plantation
1345 Carnton Lane
Franklin, TN 37064
615/794-0903

The Parthenon
Centennial Park
Nashville, TN 37209
615/862-8431

TEXAS

Bayou Bend Collections
1 Westcott St.
Houston, TX 77027
713/639-7750

VIRGINIA

Arlington House
George Washington
Memorial Pkwy.
McLean, VA 22101
703/557-0613

Ash Lawn–Highland
Route 6, Box 37
James Monroe Pkwy.
Charlottesville, VA 22902
804/293-9539

Belle Grove Plantation
336 Belle Grove Rd.
Middletown, VA 22645
540/869-2028

Carter's Grove
Colonial Williamsburg
8797 Pocahontas Trail
Williamsburg, VA 23185
757/229-1000

Colonial Williamsburg
Foundation
134 N. Henry St.
Williamsburg, VA 23185
757/229-1000

Monticello
Route 53 East
Charlottesville, VA 22902
804/984-9822

Montpelier
11407 Constitution Highway
Montpelier Station, VA 22957
540/672-2728

Mount Vernon
George Washington Pkwy.
Mount Vernon, VA 22121
703/780-2000

Oatlands Plantation
20850 Oatlands
Plantation Lane
Leesburg, VA 20175
703/777-3174

Pope-Leighey House
9000 Richmond Highway
Alexandria, VA 22309
703/780-4000

Stratford Hill Plantation
Stratford, VA 22558
804/493-8038

Woodlawn Plantation,
National Trust for
Historic Preservation
9000 Richmond Highway
Alexandria, VA 22309
703/780-4000

Resources

ALABAMA

Antiques

BIRMINGHAM

Bradshaw House Gallery
205/933-2121

Bridges Antiques
205/967-6233

The Chinaberry
205/879-5338

The Garage
205/252-1515

Hen House Antiques
205/918-0505

Interiors Market
205/323-2817

The King's House Antiques
205/871-5787

Lot Fifty-Five
205/879-0551

Mary Adams Antiques
205/871-7131

Mary Helen McCoy Fine
Antiques & Interiors
205/870-4777

Wardemond Jackson Galleries
205/871-0433

FAIRHOPE

Bountiful Home
334/990-8655

Christine's By-the-Bay
334/990-0588

Crown & Colony Antiques
334/928-4808

Past Pleasures
334/928-8484

MONTGOMERY

Herron House Antiques
334/265-2063

Pickwick Antiques
334/279-1481

Whimsey Inc.
334/262-7522

Home Furnishings and Accessories

BIRMINGHAM

A Mano
205/871-9093

At Home
205/879-3510

The Briarcliff Shop
205/870-8110

Christine's
205/871-8297

The Dandé Lion
205/879-0691

Hotel Brazil
205/879-8731

Marguerite's Conceits
205/879-2730

Renaissance Interiors
205/871-8138

Richard Tubb Interiors
205/324-7613

Table Matters
205/879-0125

Three Sheets
205/871-2337

Villa Nova
205/870-3400

FAIRHOPE

Iron-Age Gallery
334/990-5351

HUNTSVILLE

Lawren's
256/534-4428

Topiary Tree
256/536-7800

Garden Shops

BIRMINGHAM

Charlotte & Company Inc.
205/967-3163

Christopher Glenn Inc.
205/870-1236

The Elegant Earth
205/870-3264

NORTHPORT

The Potager
205/752-4761

ARKANSAS

Antiques

LITTLE ROCK

Antiquarius
501/666-0339

The Bursary
501/664-1163

Grand Finale
501/661-9242

Marshall Clements
501/663-1828

Home Furnishings and Accessories

FAYETTEVILLE

Beauregard
501/521-2592

LITTLE ROCK

Dauphine Interior Designs
501/664-6007

Randall's Fine Linens
501/664-1008

DISTRICT OF COLUMBIA

Antiques

Andrew Leddy & Co.
202/638-5394

David Bell Antiques
202/965-2355

Frank Milwee Antiques
202/333-4811

Gore Dean
202/625-1776

Hastening Antiques Ltd.
202/333-7662

Marston Luce
202/775-9460

Susquehanna Antique
Company Inc.
202/333-1511

Home Furnishings and Accessories

A Mano
202/298-7200

August Georges
202/337-5110

Baldaquin
202/625-1600

Corso De' Fiori
202/628-1929

Cynthia P. Reed Ltd.
202/333-8737

Miller and Arney
202/338-2369

Oliver-Dunn Home
Furnishings
202/686-8548

FLORIDA

Antiques

JACKSONVILLE

Simply Silver
800/731-5675

NAPLES

Les Anges Antiques
941/262-5859

PALM BEACH

Fleur-de-Lis Antiques
561/655-2295

Grand Armée
561/835-1958

Island Trading Company
561/833-0555

Letitia Lundeen Antiques
561/833-1087

The Meissen Shop
561/832-2504

SARASOTA

Bacon & Wing
941/371-2687

Jack Vinales Antiques
941/957-0002

Kevin L. Perry Inc.
941/366-8483

The Yellow Bird Antiques
941/388-1823

WEST PALM BEACH

N. P. Trent Antiques
561/832-0919

Home Furnishings and Accessories

AVENTURA

Nu-D-Zine
305/936-0079

CORAL GABLES

J. Vincent
305/445-8381

MIAMI BEACH

Details at Home
305/531-1325

Dish
305/532-7737

South Beach Style
305/538-8277

NAPLES

Le Cherche-Midi
941/263-7999

Summerfields
941/430-2505

Devonshire
561/835-4777
Kemble Interiors
561/659-5556
Mary Mahoney
561/655-8288

SARASOTA

Moore & Peters
941/955-3546
Sarasota Trading Co.
941/953-7776

SEASIDE

L. Pizitz
850/231-2240

WEST PALM BEACH

Incurable Collector
561/655-9791

Garden Shops

NAPLES

Chelsea Gardens
941/263-0520
Devonshire
941/643-5888
Twigs
941/262-8944

SARASOTA

The Elegant Earth
941/953-3339

GEORGIA

Antiques

ATLANTA

Acquisitions
404/261-2478
or 404/237-8414
Beverly Bremer Silver Shop
404/261-4009
The Gables Antiques
404/231-0734
H. Moog
404/351-2200
Interiors Market
404/352-0055
Jane J. Marsden Antiques
& Interiors
404/355-1288
Levison and Cullen Gallery
404/351-3435
Maison de Provence
404/364-0205
Randall Tysinger Antiques
404/261-7170

Regalo Antiques
404/237-4899
Regen-Leigh Antiques
404/262-9303
The Stalls on Bennett Street
404/352-4430
Travis Antiques & Interiors
404/233-7207
20th Century Antiques
404/892-2065
William Word Antiques
404/233-6890

SAVANNAH

Alex Raskin Antiques
912/232-8205
Arthur Smith Antiques
912/236-9701
Fran Campbell Antiques
912/238-5400
Simply Silver
912/238-3652

*Home Furnishings
and Accessories*

ATLANTA

Axis Twenty
404/261-4022
Belle Chambre
404/816-5333
C'est Moi
404/467-0095
Eclectic Electric
404/875-2840
Flack's Interiors
404/816-1722
Glyn Weakley, Ltd.
404/841-6649
Lush Life Home
404/233-6882
Paces Papers
404/231-1111
Pierre Deux
404/869-7790
Plantation Shop
404/239-1866
Raison D'etre Inc.
404/816-2828
Van Tosh & Associates
404/888-0613
The Wrecking Bar
404/525-0468

Garden Shops

ATLANTA

Boxwoods Gardens & Gifts
404/233-3400
Lush Life
404/841-9661

Ryan Gainey & Company
404/233-2050

KENTUCKY

Antiques

LOUISVILLE

Bittners
502/584-6349
Isaacs & Isaacs
502/897-2232
Trace Mayer Antiques
502/899-5335

SHELBYVILLE

Wakefield-Scearce
Galleries Inc.
502/633-4382

LOUISIANA

Antiques

BATON ROUGE

Beth Claybourn Interiors
225/751-3466
Fireside Antiques
225/752-9565
Inessa Stewart's Antiques
225/769-9363

BREAUX BRIDGE

Au Vieux Paris Antiques
318/332-2852

NEW ORLEANS

Animal Art Antiques
504/529-4407
Ann Koerner Antiques
504/899-2664
As You Like It Silver Shop
800/828-2311
Au Vieux Paris Antiques
504/866-6677
Bienville Shop and Gallery
504/529-2300
Blackamoor Antiques Inc.
504/523-7786
Brass Monkey
504/561-0688
Bremermann Designs
504/891-7763
Bush Antiques
504/581-3518
Charbonnet & Charbonnet
504/891-9948
Collections II
504/523-2000

Diane Genre Oriental
Art & Antiques
504/595-8945
Didier Antiques
504/899-7749
Dixon & Dixon
800/848-5148
Empire Antiques
504/897-0252
French Collectibles
504/897-9020
Gerald D. Katz Antiques
504/524-5050
Harris Antiques Ltd.
504/523-1605
Jean Bragg Antiques
504/895-7375
Jon Antiques
504/899-4482
Keil's Antiques
504/522-4552
Kurt E. Schon Ltd.
504/524-5462
Lucullus
504/528-9620
Mac Maison Ltd.
504/891-2863
Manheim Galleries
504/568-1901
Moss Antiques
504/522-3981
M. S. Rau Inc.
800/544-9440
Passages Antiques
504/899-3883
Ray J. Piehet Antiques
504/525-2806
Regency House Antiques
504/524-7507
Renaissance Shop
504/525-8568
Robinson's Antiques
504/523-6683
Royal Antiques
504/524-7033
Uptowner Antiques
504/891-7700
Waldhorn & Adler's
800/925-7912
Whisnant Galleries
504/524-9766
Wirthmore Antiques
504/269-0660

*Home Furnishings
and Accessories*

BATON ROUGE

Villa Vici
225/927-5051

NEW ORLEANS

Angèle Parlange Design
504/897-6511

artSmart Inc.
504/891-0110

Aux Belles Choses
504/891-1009

The Curtain Exchange
504/897-2444

Erica Larkin Studio
504/488-2884

GB
504/899-0212

Jacqueline Vance Rugs
504/891-3304

Orient Expressed
504/899-3060

Pied Nu
504/899-4118

Scriptura
504/897-1555

Shop of the Two Sisters
504/524-6213

Sister Agnes
504/269-9444

305 Shop
504/525-0327

Villa Vici
504/899-2931

MARYLAND

Antiques

ANNAPOLIS

DHS Designs
410/280-3466

BALTIMORE

Amos Judd & Son
410/462-2000

Crosskeys Antiques
410/728-0101

Imperial Half Bushel
410/462-1192

CHEVY CHASE

Lomax Schinzel Antiques
301/656-1911

KENSINGTON

Sparrows
301/530-0175

SAVAGE

E. J. Grant Antiques
301/953-9292

*Home Furnishings
and Accessories*

ANNAPOLIS

Bishop's Gate
410/280-3324

Interior Concepts Collection
410/263-2213

Plat du Jour
410/269-1499

BETHESDA

Ancient Rhythms
301/652-2669

Well-Furnished
Home & Garden
301/469-0268

MISSISSIPPI

Antiques

JACKSON

Interiors Market
601/981-6020

*Home Furnishings
and Accessories*

JACKSON

Annelle Primos & Associates
601/362-6154

The Elephant's Ear
601/982-5140

OXFORD

Inside Oxford
601/234-1444

Weather Vane
601/236-1120

Garden Shops

OXFORD

Oxford Floral
601/234-2515

NORTH CAROLINA

Antiques

BLOWING ROCK

Family Heirlooms
828/295-0090

Windwood Antiques
828/295-9260

CHAPEL HILL

Whitehall at the Villa
919/942-3179

CHARLOTTE

Circa Interiors & Antiques
704/332-1668

The Crescent Collection Ltd.
704/333-7922

The English Room
704/377-3625

Mary Frances Miller
Antiques & Interiors
704/375-9240

Queen Charlotte Antiques
704/333-0472

GREENSBORO

Caroline Faison Antiques
336/272-0261

HIGHLANDS

A Country Home
828/526-9038

Lyn K. Holloway Antiques
828/743-2524

*Home Furnishings
and Accessories*

BLOWING ROCK

Celeste's Interiors
828/295-3481

Feather Your Nest
828/295-0708

CHARLOTTE

Bedside Manor
704/554-7727

Ciel Home
704/372-3335

Eclectix
704/372-8485

Interiors Marketplace
704/377-6226

Jenko's
704/375-1779

N-Squared
704/333-9593

HIGH POINT

Randall Tysinger Antiques
336/883-4477

PITTSBORO

Dovecote
919/542-1145

RALEIGH

Hayes & Blume
919/832-6680

Garden Shops

CHARLOTTE

Charlotte's Garden
704/333-5353

GASTONIA

Climbing the Walls
704/852-3848

SOUTH CAROLINA

Antiques

BEAUFORT

Michael Rainey Antiques
843/521-4532

CHARLESTON

Architrave Antiques
843/577-2860

A'riga IV Antiques
843/577-3075

Church Street Galleries
843/934-0808

Century House Antiques
843/722-6248

Chicora Antiques
843/722-0640

D. Bigda Antiques
843/722-0248

English Patina Antiques
843/853-0380

Estate Antiques
843/723-2362

Helen Martin Antiques
843/577-6533

The Ginkgo Leaf
843/722-0640

Golden & Associates Antiques
843/723-8886

Jack Patla Company
843/723-2314

Livingston's Antiques
843/556-6162

Mary Clowney Antiques
& Interiors
843/853-6119

Moore House Antiques
843/722-8065

152 AD
843/577-7042

Shalimar Antiques
843/766-1529

Verdi Antiques
843/723-3953

*Home Furnishings
and Accessories*

CHARLESTON

Blink
843/577-5688

Christian Michi
843/723-0575

The Ground Floor
843/722-3576

Nina Liu & Friends
843/722-2724

COLUMBIA

Eclexion
803/799-0300

Mais Oui
803/733-1704

Verve
803/799-0045

TENNESSEE

Antiques

NASHVILLE

Cinnamon Hill Antiques
615/352-6608

Evelyn Anderson Galleries
615/352-6770

Garden Park Antiques
615/254-1996

*Home Furnishings
and Accessories*

NASHVILLE

Bella Linea
615/352-4041

Made in France
615/329-9300

Street Smart
615/329-9337

Garden Shops

NASHVILLE

Botanica
615/386-3839

The Tulip Tree
615/352-1466

TEXAS

Antiques

AUSTIN

James Powell Antiques
512/477-9939

Whit Hanks Antiques
512/478-2101

DALLAS

All the Comforts of Home
214/363-1745

Canterbury Antiques
214/821-5265

East & Orient
214/741-1191

French Homestead
214/744-0260

Heritage Collection
214/871-0012

Inessa Stewart's Antiques
214/366-2660

Le Louvre French Antiques
214/742-2605

Loyd Paxton
214/521-1521

Maison de France/
The Victory
214/742-1222

The Mews
214/748-9070

Le Passé French Antiques
214/956-9320

Raymond Pittet & Co.
214/748-8999

The Whimsey Shoppe
214/824-6300

HOUSTON

Brian Stringer Antiques
713/526-7380

Carl Moore Antiques
713/524-2502

Jas A. Gundry, Inc.
713/524-6622

John Holt Antiques
& Primitives
713/528-5065

Kay O'Toole Antiques
& Eccentricities
713/523-1921

Phyllis Tucker Antiques
713/524-0165

R. N. Wakefield & Co.
713/528-4677

W. Graham Arader III
713/621-7151

*Home Furnishings
and Accessories*

DALLAS

Amen Wardy
214/522-6763

Jan Showers
214/747-5252

The Linen Gallery
214/522-6700

The Mews
214/748-9070

Notable Accents
214/369-5525

Out of Africa
214/373-4802

Past Perfect
214/744-5717

Stanley Korshak
214/871-3608

Translations
214/373-8391

Uncommon Market
214/871-2775

FORT WORTH

Strings
817/336-8042

FREDERICKSBURG

Homestead
830/997-5551

HOUSTON

Area
713/528-0220

Events
713/520-5700

Krispen
713/621-4404

Longoria Collection
713/467-8495

Victoria's Fine Linens
713/840-8558

Watkins, Schatte, Culver
& Gardner
713/529-0597

SAN ANTONIO

Hanley-Wood
210/822-3311

Horse of a Different Color
210/824-9762

ZaZu
210/828-9838

Garden Shops

BRENHAM

Margaret Shanks Garden
Antiques & Ornaments
409/830-0606

DALLAS

Avant Garden
214/559-3432

Rolston & Bonick,
Antiques for the Garden
214/826-7775

HOUSTON

The Garden Gate
713/528-2654

VIRGINIA

Antiques

ALEXANDRIA

Sumpter Priddy III Inc.
703/299-0800

Woldman & Woldman
703/548-3122

CHARLOTTESVILLE

Kenny Ball Antiques
804/293-1361

1740 House Antiques
804/977-1740

MIDDLEBURG

Hastening Antiques Ltd.
540/687-5664

Wickets
540/687-5505

RICHMOND

Kim Faison Antiques
804/282-3736

Robert Blair Antiques
& Interior Design
804/285-9441

*Home Furnishings
and Accessories*

CHARLOTTESVILLE

Terracottage
804/923-3913

Garden Shops

MIDDLEBURG

Devonshire
540/687-5990

WEST VIRGINIA

Antiques

SHEPHERDSTOWN

Matthews & Shank Antiques
304/876-6550

Southern
Museums

ALABAMA

Birmingham Museum of Art
2000 8th Ave. N
Birmingham, AL 35203
205/254-2565

Huntsville Museum of Art
300 Church St.
Huntsville, AL 35801
256/535-4350

Mobile Museum of Art
4850 Museum Dr.
Mobile, AL 36608
334/343-2667

Montgomery Museum
of Fine Arts
1 Museum Dr.
Montgomery, AL 36117
334/244-5700

ARKANSAS

Arkansas Arts Center
9th St. & Commerce St.
Little Rock, AR 72203
501/372-4000

Decorative Arts Museum
7th & Rock
Little Rock, AR 72201
501/396-0357

DELAWARE

Winterthur Museum,
Garden, and Library
Route 52
Winterthur, DE 19735
302/888-4600

DISTRICT OF COLUMBIA

Arthur M. Sackler Gallery
Smithsonian Institution
1050 Independence Ave., SW
Washington, DC 20540
202/357-2700

Corcoran Gallery of Art
510 17th St., NW
Washington, DC 20006
202/638-3211

The Freer Gallery of Art
Smithsonian Institution
Jefferson Dr. & 12th St., SW
Washington, DC 20560
202/357-2104

Hillwood Museum
4155 Linnean Ave., NW
Washington, DC 20008
202/686-8500

Hirshhorn Museum
and Sculpture Garden
Smithsonian Institution
Independence Ave.
& 8th St., SW
Washington, DC 20560
202/357-2600

National Gallery of Art
401 Constitution Ave., NW
Washington, DC 20565
202/737-4215

The National Museum
of African Art
Smithsonian Institution
8th & G Sts., NW
Washington, DC 20560
202/357-2700

The National Museum
of American Art
Smithsonian Institution
8th & G Sts., NW
Washington, DC 20560
202/357-2700

The National Museum
of Women in the Arts
1250 New York Ave., NW
Washington, DC 20005
202/783-7370

National Portrait Gallery
Smithsonian Institution
8th & F Sts., NW
Washington, DC 20560
203/357-2700

The Phillips Collection
1600 21st St., NW
Washington, DC 20009
202/387-2151

Renwick Gallery
Smithsonian Institution
Pennsylvania Ave.
& 17th St., NW
Washington, DC 20560
202/357-2700

The Textile Museum
2320 S St., NW
Washington, DC 20008
202/667-0441

FLORIDA

Boca Raton Museum of Art
801 W. Palmetto Park Rd.
Boca Raton, FL 33486
561/392-2500

Cummer Museum
of Art and Gardens
829 Riverside Ave.
Jacksonville, FL 32204
904/356-6857

The Jacksonville Museum
of Contemporary Art
4160 Boulevard Center Dr.
Jacksonville, FL 32207
904/398-8336

Miami Art Museum
101 W. Flagler St.
Miami, FL 33130
305/375-3000

Museum of Art,
Fort Lauderdale
1 E. Las Olas Blvd.
Fort Lauderdale, FL 33301
954/525-5500

Norton Museum of Art
1451 S. Olive Ave.
W. Palm Beach, FL 33333
561/832-5196

Orlando Museum of Art
2416 N. Mills Ave.
Orlando, FL 32803
407/896-4231

Tampa Museum of Art
600 N. Ashley Dr.
Tampa, FL 33602
813/274-8130

GEORGIA

High Museum of Art
1280 Peachtree St., NE
Atlanta, GA 30309
404/733-4444

Michael C. Carlos Museum
Emory University
571 S. Kilgo St.
Atlanta, GA 30322
404/727-4282

Morris Museum of Art
1 10th St.
Augusta, GA 30901-1134
706/724-7501

Museum of Arts and Sciences
4182 Forsyth Rd.
Macon, GA 31210
912/477-3232

Telfair Academy of Arts
and Sciences
121 Barnard St.
Savannah, GA 31401
912/232-1177

KENTUCKY

Kentucky Art and Craft
Foundation Gallery
609 W. Main St.
Louisville, KY 40202
502/589-0102

The Speed Art Museum
2035 South 3rd St.
Louisville, KY 40201-2600
502/634-2700

LOUISIANA

Historic New Orleans
Collection
533 Royal St.
New Orleans, LA 70130
504/523-4662

Louisiana State Museum
751 Chartres St.
New Orleans, LA 70116
504/568-6968

New Orleans Museum of Art
1 Collins Diboll Circle
New Orleans, LA 70179
504/488-2631

MARYLAND

Baltimore Museum of Art
10 Art Museum Dr.
Baltimore, MD 21218
410/396-6300

The Walters Art Gallery
600 N. Charles St.
Baltimore, MD 21201
410/547-9000

MISSISSIPPI

Lauren Rogers Museum of Art
5th Ave. & 7th St.
Laurel, MS 39440
601/649-6374

Meridian Museum of Art
25th Ave. & 7th St.
Meridian, MS 39301
601/693-1501

George E. Ohr Arts
& Cultural Center
136 George E. Ohr St.
Biloxi, MS 39530
228/374-5547

Mississippi Museum of Art
201 E. Pascagoula St.
Jackson, MS 39201
601/960-1515

Walter Anderson
Museum of Art
510 Washington Ave.
Ocean Springs, MS 39564
228/872-3164

NORTH CAROLINA

Ackland Art Museum
University of North Carolina
Chapel Hill, NC 27599-3400
919/966-5736

Asheville Art Museum
2 S. Pack Square
Asheville, NC 28802
828/253-3227

Duke University
Museum of Art
Duke University
Durham, NC 27708
919/684-5135

Mint Museum of Art
2730 Randolph Rd.
Charlotte, NC 28207
704/337-2000

Mint Museum
of Craft and Design
220 N. Tryon St.
Charlotte, NC 28202
704/337-2079

Museum of Early Southern
Decorative Art (MESDA)
924 S. Main St.
Winston-Salem, NC 27101
336/721-7360

North Carolina
Museum of Art
2110 Blue Ridge Rd.
Raleigh, NC 27607
919/833-1935

Southeastern Center for
Contemporary Art (SECCA)
750 Marguerite Dr.
Winston-Salem, NC 27106
336/725-1904

OKLAHOMA

Gilcrease Museum
1400 Gilcrease Museum Rd.
Tulsa, OK 74127
918/596-2700

Philbrook Museum
of Fine Arts
2727 S. Rockford Rd.
Tulsa, OK 74152-0510
918/749-7941

SOUTH CAROLINA

Columbia Museum of Art
1112 Bull St.
Columbia, SC 29201
803/799-2810

Gibbes Museum of Art
135 Meeting St.
Charleston, SC 29401
803/722-2706

Greenville County
Museum of Art
420 College St.
Greenville, SC 29601
864/271-7570

TENNESSEE

Cheekwood Museum
1200 Forrest Park Dr.
Nashville, TN 37205
615/356-8000

Dixon Gallery and Gardens
4339 Park Ave.
Memphis, TN 38117
901/761-5250

Hunter Museum
of American Art
10 Bluff View
Chattanooga, TN 37403
423/267-0968

Knoxville Museum of Art
1050 World's Fair Park Dr.
Knoxville, TN 37916
423/525-6101

Memphis Brooks
Museum of Art
1934 Poplar Ave.
Memphis, TN 38104
901/722-3500

TEXAS

Amon Carter Museum
3501 Camp Bowie Blvd.
Fort Worth, TX 76107
817/738-1933

Austin Museum of Art—
Laguna Gloria
3809 W. 35th St.
Austin, TX 78703
512/458-8191

Dallas Museum of Art
1717 N. Harwood
Dallas, TX 75201
214/922-1200

Jack S. Blanton
Museum of Art
University of Texas
23rd & San Jacinto
Austin, TX 78712-1205
512/471-7324

Kimbell Art Museum
3333 Camp Bowie Blvd.
Fort Worth, TX 76107
817/332-8451

McNay Art Museum
6000 N. New Braunfels
San Antonio, TX 78209
210/824-5368

The Menil Collection
1515 Sul Ross
Houston, TX 77006
713/525-9400

Modern Art Museum
of Fort Worth
1309 Montgomery St.
Fort Worth, TX 76107
817/738-9215

The Museum of Fine Arts,
Houston
1001 Bissonnet
Houston, TX 77005
713/639-7300

Museums of Abilene
102 Cypress St.
Abilene, TX 79601
915/673-4587

VIRGINIA

Abby Aldrich Rockefeller
Folk Art Center
307 S. England St.
Williamsburg, VA 23185
804/229-1000, ext. 7670

The Chrysler Museum
245 W. Olney Rd.
Norfolk, VA 28510-1587
757/664-6200

Colonial Williamsburg
Foundation
134 N. Henry St.
Williamsburg, VA 23185
757/229-1000

Marsh Art Gallery
University of Richmond
Richmond, VA 23173
804/289-8276

Virginia Museum of Fine Arts
2800 Grove Ave.
Richmond, VA 23221-2466
804/367-0844

WEST VIRGINIA

Huntington Museum of Art
2033 McCoy Rd.
Huntington, WV 25701
304/529-2701

Acknowledgments

INTERIOR SPACES

Sylvia Atchison, Atchison Imports, 921 Dauphin St., Mobile, AL 36604, 334/438-4800: 36R, 38–39, 59T

Gerrie Bremermann, Bremermann Designs, 3943 Magazine St., New Orleans, LA 70115, 504/891-7763: 100

Brown-Davis Interiors, 1617 29th St., NW, Washington, DC 20007, 202/333-5883: 43, 120

Dan Carithers, 2300 Peachtree Rd., NW, Suite B-201, Atlanta, GA 30309, 404/355-8661: 20, 24, 26, 28T, 35B, 62, 99, 128

Barbara Carlton, Shabby Slips, 2304 Bissonnet, Houston, TX 77005, 713/630-0066: 52, 91, 124, 126–27

Granger Carr, McAlpine, Booth & Carr Interiors Inc., 644 South Perry St., Montgomery, AL 36106, 334/262-5556: 36L, 60

Anne Charlton, 41 Paradise Walk, London SW3 4JL, England, 011-44-171-349-0515: 18, 118L

John Chrestia, Chrestia Staub Pierce, 7219 Perrier St., New Orleans, LA 70118, 504/866-6677: 33, 122B

Jane Churchill, Jane Churchill Interiors Ltd., 81 Pimlico Rd., London SW1W 8PH, England, 011-44-171-730-8564: 29

Joseph Paul Davis Interior Design, 1519 Connecticut Ave., NW, Suite 200, Washington, DC 20036, 202/328-1717: 5, 48

Barry Dixon, Inc., 2019 Q St., NW, Washington, DC 20009, 202/332-7955: 56, 125R

Mary Douglas Drysdale, Drysdale Design Associates, 1733 Connecticut Ave., NW, Washington, DC 20009, 202/588-0700: 34B, 55, 65B, 129

Patrick Dunne, Lucullus, 610 Chartres St., New Orleans, LA 70130, 504/528-9620: 30, 31, 37, 70–71, 82B, 108

Gandy/Peace, 349 Peachtree Hills Ave., NE, Suite C2, Atlanta, GA 30305, 404/237-8681: 90, 105

Jennifer Garrigues Inc., 308 Peruvian Ave., Palm Beach, FL 33480, 561/659-7085: 68, 95, 101

Renée Green Interior Design, 137 Strand St., Santa Monica, CA 90405, 310/314-4065: 64B

Sam Greeson, Meyer-Greeson-Paullin, 320 S. Tryon St., Suite 222, Charlotte, NC 28202, 704/375-1001: 93L

Trudy Hurley, Green Parrot Interiors, 305 Duplessis St., Metairie, LA 70005, 504/834-8029: 75

Susan Hurwitt Design, 3 Cook St., Rowayton, CT 06853, 203/853-2717: 58B, 59B, 77

Michael Imber Architect, 111 West El Prado, San Antonio, TX 78212, 210/824-7703: 64B

Cathy Kincaid Interiors, 4504 Mockingbird Lane, Dallas, TX 75205, 214/522-0856: 2, 28B, 44

Bobby McAlpine, McAlpine Tankersley Architecture Inc., 644 South Perry St., Montgomery, AL 36104, 334/262-8315: 49, 58B, 59B, 67, 77, 92

Hilton McConnico, 8 rue Antoine Panier, 93170 Bajnolet, France: 54, 98, 106

Bill McGee, Alexander Baer Associates, Inc., 24 West Chase St., Baltimore, MD 21201, 410/727-4100: 22, 27, 76, 88, 103T, 107

J. R. Miller Design Middleburg, 17586 Raven Rock Rd., Bluemont, VA 22012, 540/554-8400: 94

David Mitchell Interior, 1734 Connecticut Ave., NW, Washington, DC 20024, 202/797-0780: 74, 109, 125L

Nancy Morton and Chris Cocroft, Ginger Lily, 1121 West 11th St., Boca Grande, FL 33921, 941/964-2474: 42

Oetgen Design Inc., 2300 Peachtree Rd., NW, Atlanta, GA 30309, 404/352-1112: 45, 78, 81, 112L, 116, 121R, 121L, 122T

Betty Lou Phillips, ASID, Interiors by B.L.P., 4278 Bordeaux Ave., Dallas, TX 75205, 214/599-0191: 57

Annelle Primos & Associates, 4500 I-55 N., Highland Village, Suite 126, Jackson, MS 39211, 601/362-6154: 80

Suzanne Rheinstein, Hollyhock Design, 136½ N. Larchmont Blvd., Los Angeles, CA 90004, 213/466-0750: 21, 23, 51, 66, 72, 83T, 93R, 97, 104

Margaret Rubino, Rooms & Gardens, Inc., 290 Lafayette St., New York, NY 10012, 212/431-1297, and in Washington, DC, by appointment only, 202/362-3777: 111, 118R

Jan Showers & Associates, 1308 Slocum, Dallas, TX 75207, 214/747-5252: 79

Cindy Smith, Circa Interiors & Antiques, 2321 Crescent Ave., Charlotte, NC 28207, 704/332-1668: 58B, 59B, 77

Smith & Smith Design, 4000 Shannon Lane, Dallas, TX 75205, 214/528-2255: 50T, 50B, 84, 89L

Jose Solis Betancourt, Solis Betancourt Designs, 1054 Potomac St., NW, Washington, DC 20007, 202/659-8734: 40, 41, 96

Laurie Steichen, Steichen Interior Design, 1031 N. Hagan St., New Orleans, LA 70119, 504/484-6288: 53

Greg Tankersley, McAlpine Tankersley Architecture Inc., 644 South Perry St., Montgomery, AL 36104, 334/262-8315: 19, 64T, 83B

Susan Trowbridge, Little & Trowbridge Design Studio, Santa Fe, NM, 87501, 505/995-8214: 37, 70–71, 82B

Rebecca Turner-Wiggins, Wiggins & Associates, 3405 South Western Blvd., Dallas, TX 75225, 214/739-7096: 42, 47

ARCHITECTS

Alexander Gorlin, 137 Varick St., New York, NY 10013, 212/229-1199: 137

Cole & Cole, 3120 Zelda Ct., Montgomery, AL 36106, 334/213-0094: 134

Gandy/Peace, 349 Peachtree Hills Ave., NE, Suite C2, Atlanta, GA 30305, 404/237-8681: 149B

Grenfell Architecture, 1100 South Mint St., Suite 208, Charlotte, NC 28203, 704/372-2916: 144, 145

Harrison Design Associates, 3198 Cains Hill Place NW, Suite 200, Atlanta, GA 30305, 404/365-7760: 142

Jorge Hernandez, 7550 SW 57th Ave., Suite 211, Miami, FL 33143, 305/666-2181: 152

Ken Tate Architect, 1437 Old Square Rd., Suite 107, Jackson, MS 39211, 601/981-5586: 148T

Larry Boerder Architect, 4514 Cole, Suite 101, Dallas, TX 75205, 214/559-2285: 42, 47, 131, 149T

McAlpine Tankersley Architecture Inc., 644 South Perry St., Montgomery, AL 36104, 334/262-8315: 146T, 146B, 147

Norman Askins Architects, 2995 Lookout Place, NE, Atlanta, GA 30305, 404/233-6565: 149B

Jim Strickland, Historical Concepts, 430 Prime Point, Suite 103, Peachtree City, GA 30269, 770/487-8041: 150–51

Surber Berber Choate & Hertlein, 1776 Peachtree St., NW, Suite 700S, Atlanta, GA 30309, 404/872-8400: 140

Turner Architectural Designs, Inc., 110 Third Ave., SE, Moultrie, GA 31768, 912/985-2038: 148B

Versaci Neumann & Partners, 205 E. Washington St., Middleburg, VA 22117, 540/687-3917: 141

LANDSCAPE DESIGNERS

Norman Kent Johnson, 2215 Cahaba Rd., Birmingham, AL 35209, 205/933-6434: 172, 173, 174–75

Warren Johnson Landscape Architecture, 2613 Fallcreek Drive, Carrollton, TX 75006, 972/418-5128: 155, 163T

Steve Miller Landscape Architecture, 2201 Tucker St., Suite 104, Dallas, TX 75214, 214/327-0099: 155, 163T

Ben Page & Associates 1207 17th Ave. South, Nashville, TN 37212, 615/320-0220: 157 (text)

Jorge Sanchez, Wheelock, Sanchez & Maddux, 235 Peruvian, Palm Beach, FL 33480, 561/655-9006: 154, 177

P. Allen Smith, pallensmith. com: 170T, 170B

Picture Credits

Index

accessories, 99–128; garden room, 46; household, 14; natural, 118
Adam style, 132
Adler, Lee, 186
African–American culture, 20
Aiken, Harriet and William, 10
Aiken–Rhett mansion, 8, 9, 10, 12, 13
American Academy, Rome, 136
American Classicist: The Architecture of Philip Trammell Shutze (Dowling), 136
American Horticultural Society, 159
antique furniture, 27–28, 75, 79, 86, 95–96
antiquity, classical, 108, 181
architecture: English influence in, 132; evolution of in South, 134–42; French influence in, 132–33; Mediterranean, 131, 149; postmodern movement in, 140–41; Spanish influence in, 133; Texas, 137; tradition–based, 141–43; Tuscan–style, 43
artwork, 100–109; in bookshelves, 108; combining old and new, 104–106, 108; on patterned walls, 100. *See also* paintings
automobile, impact of, 146

barn, renovated, 34, 82
Baroque, 141–42, 145
Bartlett Yancey House, 189
baskets, antique, 72, 115, 118
Beaufort, South Carolina: preservation in, 191
Beaux Arts, 108
bedroom: Atlanta, 78; Dallas, 84; fabrics for, 81–84; Houston, 91; Maryland, 77, 88; Mississippi, 81, 82; seating areas in, 88–92; Spartanburg, South Carolina, 77; sunlight in, 78; traditional furnishings for, 13–14, 79–81, 84–86
bedsteads, 86–87; antique, 77, 95–96; canopied, 86; king-sized, 77; twin, 95
Berendt, John, 186

bicentennial celebration (1976), 189
Bloom, Julie, 109
Boerder, Larry, 149
books/bookcases, 40
Bottomley, W. L., 134
Brainard, Bruce, 105
Brewton, Alabama, 9
Briscoe, Birdsall, 134
Bureau of Public Roads, 185

Carnegie Institution, 184
central passage, as sleeping quarters, 92
ceramics, 115–16. *See also* pottery
chairs: bedroom, 90; dining room, 51, 54, 60; Louis XVI, 75; wing, 90
chaise longues, 91–92
Charleston, South Carolina, 8, 10, 77, 131; gardens in, 160–62
Charleston Single House, 131, 152
Charlottesville, Virginia, 7, 10, 21, 23, 181
Chatelaine, Verne, 184
Chestnut, Mary Boykin, 10
Chopin, Kate, 179
Civil War, 133
Coconut Grove, Florida, 155
collections, 110–18; ceramics, 89, 110, 111; eccentricity in, 117; hand-blown bottles, 112; hat molds, 40; hats, 113, 117; *National Geographic* magazines, 116, 117; plates, 65; pond yachts, 116; shoes, 113, 117; stone paintings, 103; walking sticks, 113, 117
Colonial Revival style, 193
Colonial Williamsburg, 90, 181, 193
color: accents of, 99; in Colonial Williamsburg, 193; fall, 163; in family room, 36, 40; for living rooms, 29
Conroy, Pat, 7
corona, 86
courtyard, 138, 160
craftsmanship, 111, 113
Creole style, 37, 53, 138, 180; French influence on, 163
Cunningham, Ann Pamela, 179–80

Day, Thomas, 189
daybed, 92, 93
decorative painting, interior, 106, 190, 193
design: issues of, 143–46; sources of traditional, 146; of subdivisions, 146, 152
"Désirée's Baby" (Chopin), 179
dining, informal, 62–67
dining room: in Dallas, 50, 56; drama in, 61; formal, 13, 54–61; functions of, 53; in Point Clear, Alabama, 59; at South Carolina plantation, 58; in Washington, D.C., 56
distressed look, 78–79
dogtrot, 23
domestic building, characteristics of in South, 131–32
Dowling, Elizabeth, 136
draperies, outdoor, 33
dressing room, 77
duchesse, French, 93

easel, 108–109
Edwards, Emily, 183
Elizabeth I, 88
entries, 23–26. *See also* foyer
environmental movement, 189

family room, 33–42; in Baton Rouge, 35; books in, 40; in Dallas, 35; function of, 33–36; television in, 40–41; in Washington, D.C., 34
Faulkner, William, 117
Federal style, 86, 132, 179, 184, 194
floors: dining room, 60–61; garden room, 44; living room, 30
flowers: as accessories, 118–28; in bookshelves, 125; containers for, 121; for impact, 122; neutral colors in, 125–28
food, importance of in South, 49
Ford, O'Neil, 137, 140
Ford, Powell & Carson architectural firm, 140
fountains, 173, 177
foyer: Atlanta, 24; Baltimore, 23; Charlottesville, 23; Dallas, 4, 24; Point Clear, Alabama, 59
French Quarter, 183

Gainey, Ryan, 170–71
Gandy/Peace designers, 149
Garden District, New Orleans, 134
gardening, local styles of, 160–62

garden room, 14, 43–47; in Boca Grande, Florida, 43; flooring for, 44; furnishings for, 46; in Montgomery, Alabama, 18
gardens: 155–77; boxwood, 162; cottage, 159, 168; English influence on, 164–71; French influence on, 162, 163–64; importance of, 9; organic, 157; parterre, 163, 164; pests in, 170; seating for, 164, 167; textures in, 167, 168; visual surprises in, 155; water in, 173–77
Georgian style, 132
Georgian Tidewater, 18
Ghost sculpture, 156
Gone with the Wind (Mitchell), 77, 99
Gorlin, Alex, 137
Gothic Revival style, 133
Goursat, Georges, 108
grasses and mosses, 125, 128
Great Depression, 136
Great Society programs, 186
Greek Revival style, 10, 131, 133, 184
Green, Rena Maverick, 183
Grenfell, Milton, 141, 145
guest bedroom, 77, 92, 93–97
Gusler, Liza, 90–91, 92, 93–94

Harrison Design Associates, 142
Haydel, Jean Jacques, Sr., 182
Haydel, Marcellin, 182
heirlooms, in dining room, 55–56
Henry VIII, 88
Hernandez, Jorge, 152
Historic American Buildings Survey (HABS), 182–83
Historic Charleston Foundation, 8
historic districts, 146, 181–82, 189–90, 191
Historic Savannah Foundation, 186
Historic Sites Act of 1935, 183
hospitality, Southern, 93–94
Housing and Home Finance Agency, 185

Inmans, Edward, 136
interstate highway program, 185–86
Inviting Garden, The (Lacy), 157–58
Italianate style, 133

Jay, William, 193
Jefferson, Thomas, 7, 10, 23, 132, 181

Johnson, Lyndon Baines, 186
Jones, Rob, 156

Keeping Time: The History and Theory of Preservation in America (Murtagh), 186–89
kitchens, 67–69; appliances in, 68; Birmingham, 62; decoration of, 67–68; eating spots in, 66; Louisiana, 65; Montgomery, 64; San Antonio ranch, 64; South Carolina, 67; traditional, 13, 51–52
Koch, Richard, 138

Lacy, Allen, 157–58
Langham, Richard Keith, 9
Langhorne sisters, 29
Lawrence, Elizabeth, 155, 171
Lee, Harper, 7
Lee Mansion, Arlington, Virginia, 180
LeNôtre, André, 163
Lewis, Edna, 49–50
library: in Baltimore, 27; in Baton Rouge, 28
living room, 26–33, 36; Atlanta, 26; Baton Rouge, 20; Dallas, 29; formal, 13; furnishings of, 28–29; London, 29; texture in, 29; Washington, D.C., 40; window dressing for, 32
loggia, 43, 72; Dallas, 44, 46
London, flat in, 18, 29
Louis XIV, 88, 163
Louisville, Kentucky: preservation in, 191
Low Country style, 18–20

McAlpine, Bobby, 141
McAlpine-Tankersley architectural firm, 140–41, 146
McCall, Frank, Jr., 139–40, 148
McCall-Turner architectural firm, 139, 148
McConnico, Hilton, 54
Manet, Edouard, 81–84
master bedroom, 75, 78–87, 95
Maverick, Sam, 183
Melrose, Natchez, Mississippi, 136
Merrill, Scott, 142
Midnight in the Garden of Good and Evil (Berendt), 186
Miller, Katherine, 184
Mitchell, Margaret, 77, 99
Mizner, Addison, 20, 134, 136
Moe, Richard, 189-90
Monticello, 7, 10, 23, 181
Moore-Gwyn House, 186

Mount Vernon, 179–80
Mount Vernon Ladies Association of the Union, 180
Mrs. Whaley and Her Charleston Garden, 156
Murtagh, William J., 186

Natchez, Mississippi, preservation in, 183–84
National Historic Preservation Act of 1966, 186
National Park Service, 183
National Register of Historic Places, 186
National Trust for Historic Preservation, 186–89
New Deal recovery programs, 183, 184
New Orleans sitting rooms, 30, 32, 33
New South: cities of, 9; industrialism in, 103
new traditionalists, 142–45

Oak Alley Plantation, Louisiana, 132
O'Connor, Flannery, 117
Octagon, Washington, D.C., 179, 194
Oetgen, John, 142
Oglethorpe, James Edward, 186
O'Hara, Scarlett, 50, 75, *Olympia* (Manet), 84
orangeries, 43
Oushak rug, 30, 56
outdoor dining, 69–72; in Dallas, 69; natural feel of, 72; in Palm Beach, 68; in Pass Christian, Mississippi, 72; textures of, 72
Owens–Thomas House, Savannah, 142, 193

Page, Ben, 157, 167
paintings: abstract, 104–105; animal, 103; collection of stone, 103; landscape, 100, 102–103, 104; portraits, 100. *See also* artwork
Palladio, Andrea, 10
Paris, apartment in, 17, 61, 106
pattern books, 103–104
photography, 100, 109
plants: container grown, 46; regional favorite, 159
Plater-Zyberk, Duany, 152
porcelain, 29, 35, 88, 118
porches, 172–73
pottery, 65; local, 121. *See also* ceramics
preservation: beginnings of movement for, 179–90; Charleston ordinance on, 181–82, 183; and economic development, 189–90;

revolving fund for, 182, 186. *See also* restoration
Prince of Tides, The (Conroy), 7
prints: antique bird, 103; botanical, 102, 104
property rights movement, 190
Proust, Marcel, 88

Regency style, 134, 142, 193
regional revival, in architecture, 138–39, 141–43, 148
Reich, Naaman, 190
Reich–Butner House, 191
Reid, Neil, 134
religious artifacts, Mexican, 83, 87
Renoir, Auguste, 56
restoration: impact of, 190–95; urban, 14. *See also* preservation
Riverwalk, San Antonio, 183
Robinson, John, 10
Roman house, 142

Sackville-West, Vita, 164
St. Augustine, Florida, preservation in, 184
San Antonio Conservation Society, 183
San Miguel de Allende, Mexico, 72, 160
Sargent, John Singer, 100
Savage, Thomas, 8
Savannah, construction and restoration in, 14, 18, 186
Schaub, Clemens, 142
Seaside, Florida, 137, 152
seating areas, bedroom, 88–92
Shutze, Philip Trammell, 134, 136
Siddons, Anne Rivers, 7
silhouettes, cut, 100–102
silver, 111–115
Sissinghurst, 164
slave quarters, 8, 13
sleeping areas. *See* bedroom
slipcovers, 29, 60, 66, 79–81
Smith, Lee, 17
Smith, Robert, 84, 86
sofa bed, 83
"Some Notes on River Country" (Welty), 10–13, 14
South: ethnic heritage of, 18–20; history of architecture in, 131–34; openness of houses in, 146; preindustrial enclaves in, 182; romantic view of, 75–77; sense of place in, 10; weather in, 158–59
Southern art, 100. *See also* artwork
Southern Garden, A (Lawrence), 155

space: recuperative, 89; traditional interior, 145
Staub, John, 134
still-life vignettes: art in, 109; collections in, 111, 113, 117
stones, use of, 171–72
Strand district, Galveston, 186
Streetcar Named Desire, A (Williams), 77
Strickland, Jim, 152
Sunday dinner, traditional, 54
sunporch, Atlanta, 44
Surber Barber Choate & Hertlein architectural firm, 140
Swan House, 136

tabby, 140
tables: dining, 56–60; living room, 28, 36; round, 13, 56
Tate, Ken, 141, 148
Tayloe, John, III, 179
television, 40–41
terraces, 68, 171–72, 173
toile de Jouy, 75, 77, 94–95
To Kill a Mockingbird (Lee), 7
Town, A. Hays, 137–38
trees, blossoming, 162–63
tropical garden, 160, 177
Turner, Neil, 148

Udall, Stewart L., 189
urban renewal program, 185
urban sprawl, 189

Verey, Rosemary, 167
Versaci Newman & Partners architectural firm, 141
Versailles, gardens at, 163–64
Vieux Carré. *See* French Quarter
Volk, John, 134

Wade Hampton Golf Club, Cashiers, North Carolina, 140
wallpaper, hand–painted, 106–108
Warhol, Andy, 100
Washington, George, 179
water, in garden, 173–77
Welty, Eudora, 10–13, 14, 75
Whaley, Emily, 156
Whitney Plantation, 180, 181, 182, 183
Williams, Tennessee, 77
Wilson, Samuel, 138
Windsor, Florida, house type, 142
World War II, 136–37
Wyeth, Marion Syms, 134
Wythe House, Colonial Williamsburg, 193